CITYSPOTS
OSLO

Ann Burgess and Tom Burgess

Written by Ann Burgess & Tom Burgess
Original photography Ann Carroll Burgess & Tom Burgess
Front cover photography courtesy of Alamy Images

Produced by 183 Books
Design/layout/maps: Chris Lane and Lee Biggadike, Studio 183 Ltd
Editorial/project management: Stephen York

Published by Thomas Cook Publishing
A division of Thomas Cook Tour Operations Limited
PO Box 227, Units 15/16, Coningsby Road
Peterborough PE3 8SB, United Kingdom
email: books@thomascook.com
www.thomascookpublishing.com
+44 (0)1733 416477

First edition © 2006 Thomas Cook Publishing
Text © 2006 Thomas Cook Publishing
Maps © 2006 Thomas Cook Publishing
ISBN-13: 978-1-84157-585-8
ISBN-10: 1-84157-585-2
Project Editor: Kelly Anne Pipes
Production/DTP: Steven Collins

Printed and bound in Spain by GraphyCems

CONTENTS

SYMBOLS & ABBREVIATIONS

The following symbols are used throughout this book:

☎ telephone	🖷 fax	🌐 website address
@ address	⏱ opening times	⊘ public transport connections

The following symbols are used on the maps:

🄸 Tourist Information Office

✈ Airport

🅣 T-bane (underground)

Hotels and restaurants are graded by approximate price as follows:
K budget **KK** mid-range **KKK** expensive

24-HOUR CLOCK

All times in this book are given in the 24-hour clock system used widely in Europe and in most international transport timetables.

⏵ *Karl Johans Gate is Oslo's central thoroughfare*

INTRODUCING
Oslo

Introduction

Oslo, at a first glance, is somewhat like a paperback novel. It draws you in with an enticing cover and then surprises you with a fascinating tale. In this case the cover is the dramatic scenery of the Oslofjord and the story is the myriad of activities and attractions available to the visitor.

This is a city for all seasons, although the warmest and sunniest time to visit is during the long days of summer. All of Oslo seems to live outdoors at this time, with restaurants, bars and even museums keeping longer hours to satisfy both locals and visitors. Winter, though, is also a fascinating time to come to Oslo, particularly for those who enjoy the winter sports of skiing, cross-country skiing, luge, bobsleigh and skating. All of these sporting activities are within easy distance of the city centre, allowing you to spend your days in active pursuits and your evenings absorbing Oslo's cultural treasures.

Oslo was once home to playwright Henrik Ibsen, composer Edvard Grieg, violinist Ole Bull, artist Edvard Munch and sculptor Gustav Vigeland and its cultural traditions remain strong and vibrant well into the 21st century.

And don't forget the Vikings, those adventurous bad boys of the Dark to Middle Ages who were the first to scatter Norwegian traditions over a wide swath of the globe. In later years they would be followed by the likes of Amundsen and Heyerdahl, continuing the tradition of exploration in a more socially responsible fashion.

Oslo is museum central for Norway, with more than 50 different museums. Among the most famous are the Munch Museum, Fram and the Viking Ship Museum, Norwegian Folk Museum, Vigeland Sculpture Park, the Kon-tiki Museum, and the Holmenkollen ski jump, featuring the world's oldest ski museum. The compact city centre puts most of these attractions within either walking distance or just a few minutes away by a very effective public transport system.

You'll discover Oslo to be a city of contradictions. It is both adventurous and shy, exciting and sedate, urban and rural. Oslo is one of the best kept secrets of the world, but certainly destined to be a bestseller.

Akershus Slott has guarded Oslo harbour for centuries

When to go

CLIMATE & SEASONS

Oslo has four distinct seasons. Despite its northern latitude the climate is quite moderate, owing to the warming effect of the Gulf Stream, which brings warm water from the Gulf of Mexico across the Atlantic and up the Norwegian coast. Summer temperatures average about 16°C (60°F), with highs that can reach 30°C (86°F), while winter temperatures average around 0°C (32°F), but reaching as low as -20°C (-4°F). You can expect about 80–90 mm (3–3½ in.) of rain in the summer months, and about 40–50 mm (1½–2 in.) in winter.

The main tourist season is from mid-June to Mid-September. The summer season features many festivals and other events, such as plays and concerts, most of which are held outdoors. The city also has many parks and outdoor cafés to enjoy the long summer evenings. Visit ⓦ www.summeroslo.com for more information about the city's summer activities.

If you are into winter sports, especially skiing, then Oslo makes a great winter destination. The first snows fall in late November or early December, and the skiing season gets into full swing at Christmas time, lasting until April. Oslo has many kilometres of cross-country ski runs and eight alpine ski slopes within the city limits, and many more within easy reach of the city.
ⓦ www.skioslo.com will tell you all you need to know. You can also try your skills at ice skating and tobogganing.

ANNUAL EVENTS
February/March
Winter Night Festival Oslo's classical music fest is centred on the Norwegian Chamber Music Orchestra. ⓦ www.visitoslo.com

Oslo International Church Music Festival Concerts are held in Oslo Cathedral and other churches within the city during mid-March.
ⓦ www.oslokirkemusikkfestival.no

Holmenkollen Ski Festival In the second week of March, Oslo attracts skiers and ski jumpers from around the world.
ⓦ www.skiforeningen.no

World Cup Biathlon Held during the last weekend in March.
ⓦ www.skiforeningen.no

⬥ The streets are filled during the celebrations for Constitution Day

May/June

Labour Day (1 May) is a very important family holiday. Events, parades and activities, all with a family fun theme, are held throughout the country.

St Hallvard's Day (15 May) Oslo's patron saint is celebrated with concerts, theatre presentations, folklore and lots of family-oriented activities. Ⓦ www.visitoslo.com

Constitution Day (Syttende Mai) Norway's national day is celebrated across the country on 17 May. Activities include children's parades and other festivities.

Norwegian Wood Rock Festival Mid-June sees this three-day festival featuring mostly Norwegian performers, but several international stars are usually on the programme. Ⓦ www.norwegianwood.no

Oslo Gay & Lesbian Pride Week occurs during the last week of June. Events include concerts, stand up comedy, worship services, art exhibitions, photo workshops and bowling. Ⓦ www.skeivedager.no

Midsummer Night The evening of 21 June is the occasion for bonfires and celebrations throughout Norway.

July/August

Norsk Aften (Norwegian Evening) occurs daily during July and August at the Norsk Folkemuseum, and features guided tours, folk dancing and traditional Norwegian food.

Norway Cup The world's largest international football tournament for 9–18s takes place during the first week of August. Ⓦ www.norway-cup.no/uk

Oslo International Jazz Festival The premiere summer event occurs for a week in mid-August. All forms of jazz are performed, from ragtime to rap, and performers come from all over the world to participate. Ⓦ www.oslojazz.no

Oslo Chamber Music Festival Musicians from across Norway and around the world perform in various venues across the city in the middle of August. Ⓦ www.oslokammermusikkfestival.no

October/November
The Ultima Contemporary Music Festival is held during the first two weeks of October. It combines the latest in music, dance and drama in cooperation with museums and theatres. Ⓦ www.ultima.no
Oslo World Music Festival Music from around the world is heard on various stages and venues in the city. Ⓦ www.worldmusic.no

December
Nobel Peace Prize Award Parades and many other festivities are held in honour of the annual winner of the Nobel Peace Prize. Past artists performing have included Diana Krall, Andrea Bocelli, Cyndi Lauper and Patti LaBelle. Ⓦ www.nobel.no

---

PUBLIC HOLIDAYS
Public transport runs to Sunday schedules, and banks, post offices and public buildings are closed on these days. Many shops (but not generally restaurants) will also be closed.
New Year's Day 1 Jan
Maundy Thursday, Good Friday &Easter Monday Mar/Apr
Labour Day 1 May
Constitution Day 17 May
Ascension Day 40 days after Easter, May/Jun
Whit Monday (Pentecost) eighth Monday after Easter, May/Jun
Christmas 25 and 26 Dec

Christmas in Oslo

Christmas time, or *Jul* as it is called in Norway, is a very special time of year. Jul started out as a pagan fertility feast before becoming a Christian holiday. Similarly, an imaginary Viking gnome, called *nisse*, who brought good luck to pagan farmers, has been changed into a modern day Santa Claus, or *Jule-nissen* as the locals call him. The lighting of the city's official Christmas tree at University Square on Karl Johans Gate, on the first Sunday of Advent, heralds the start of the holiday season in Oslo. It is also when the skating rink in the city centre is opened. For the entire month of December you will find the city bedecked in holiday lights and seasonal good spirits.

Pretty as the city centre may be, the holiday heart of Oslo is at the Norwegian Folk Museum on the Bygdøy peninsula. Held among the many historic buildings of the museum, the Christmas fair is a charming holiday experience. Create a gift in Santa's Workshop, join carollers along the winding paths and attend a service in the old Stave Church. Interspersed among the museum buildings you will find market stalls filled with crafts, decorations and seasonal foods. You'll also find traditional Christmas festivities at Bogstad Manor in Frogner and Baerums Verk. At the manor the main building is decorated in the style of the 19th century. Inside the museum shop you'll discover an array of unusual gifts and the café offers tastes of the season. At Baerums Verk you can ride in a horse-drawn sleigh or stroll the surroundings of this 17th-century iron mill. The old workers' houses have been converted into small shops selling hand-blown glass, pottery and woven and knitted items. You can even try your hand at creating your own Christmas decorations.

▶ *Christmas in Oslo – it's cold but it's festive*

History

Although the history of Norway and its 'Norsemen' is a violent one, the history of Oslo itself is relatively quiet and peaceful. The Vikings had been plundering and pillaging for nearly three hundred years when Oslo was founded around AD1000 by King Harald Hardrada. The name derives from two Old Norse words, 'As' the Norse god, and 'Lo' for field. Roughly translated, Oslo means 'the pasture of the gods'.

By 1300, the city had only 3000 inhabitants, but was made the seat of the royal throne of King Haakon V, and consequently, emerged as a centre of power. It was Haakon who started building Akershus Castle, which remains today. The Black Death struck in 1349 and killed over half of the population of Norway. Through royal marriages, Norway was joined to Denmark in 1380, with the Danes essentially ruling Norway for the next 400 or so years. Norway was a Catholic country until 1537, when the state religion became Evangelical Lutheran by royal decree. In 1624, Oslo was destroyed by fire. It was rebuilt by King Christian IV of Denmark, who renamed the city Christiania, after himself.

As a consequence of the Napoleonic wars, Norway was ceded to Sweden in 1814, with Christiania officially becoming its capital. Although under Swedish rule, Norway established a degree of democratic rule regarding domestic matters. For some reason, in 1877, the spelling of the city's name was changed to Kristiania, reverting to its original name of Oslo again in 1925.

In 1901, the home of the Nobel Peace Prize was moved to Oslo. After years of struggle for independence, the union with Sweden was dissolved peacefully in 1905, and Norway became a fully democratic constitutional hereditary monarchy. Norway stayed out of World War I, although she lost half of her merchant fleet in the struggle. However, although Norway declared neutrality at the start of World War II, Germany invaded In 1940 and set up a puppet government under Vidkun Quisling. The exploits of the Norwegian resistance movement are legendary, and the execution of many Norwegian patriots took place in Akershus Castle. At the end of the war, the Germans surrendered to the Norwegian resistance movement at Akershus Castle, and Quisling was imprisoned there.

Following the war, Oslo and the rest of Norway prospered. A strong fishing industry and North Sea oil have kept the economy booming. Today, Norway is one of the world's wealthiest nations per head of population Although an active member of both NATO and the United Nations, to date an independently minded Norway has stayed out of the European Union.

ST HALLVARD

The patron saint of Oslo is St Hallvard, a young Norwegian of royal descent who sacrificed his life in a deed of valour some 900 years ago. According to the legend, Hallvard tried to save a pregnant woman who was fleeing from assailants who had accused her of theft. He rowed her out into the fjord, but was unable to escape the pursuers, who killed them both. The killers put a millstone around Hallvard's neck, and sank his body in the fjord. However, the body rose to the surface with the millstone still around his neck. This miracle led to Hallvard's canonisation. Today, St Hallvard, shown holding a millstone in his right hand, is the main icon in the city of Oslo's Coat of Arms

Lifestyle

Norwegians today experience one of the highest standards of living in the world but it wasn't always so. Just a little over 50 years ago Norway was one of the poorest countries in Western Europe. Then, in the late 1960s oil was discovered in the North Sea and Norway underwent a spectacular economic reversal of fortune.

The Norwegians are a conundrum. They can be simultaneously independent and yet heavily reliant on government social programs. They are curious about the world, but reluctant to join the European Union. Eminently fair-minded, but wary of strangers, Norwegians frequently even see themselves as a bundle of contradictions.

One thing almost all Norwegians have in common is their love of the outdoors. They take the *allemansgratten* or 'every man's right' very seriously. This is the rule that allows all public access to wilderness lands. During the very short summer months there is a frenetic urge to engage in any and all kinds of outdoor activities. That doesn't mean that they spend their winters locked up inside their homes. If that were the case they wouldn't have ever developed skiing or become so expert at other winter sports. But the long dark winters in Northern latitudes do make them long for the sun.

Norwegians are also among the best educated people on the planet. Education is both compulsory and heavily funded. There is a wide range of educational programs available to students from traditional academic programs to vocational trades – and all of these programs are free. The citizens of Norway lead a very comfortable life. Although heavily taxed they enjoy a vast range of benefits including paid vacations, free medical care, free university tuition, and a lifetime retirement pension. Because of Norway's social programs, with family allowances and generous parental leave policies, it is a very good place to raise a family. Simultaneously, Norway is experiencing the problems of an ageing population

Norway is a country with no external debt. Little wonder it can occasionally flaunt world opinion, as in the case of its whaling policies. It will be interesting to watch how Norway, having just marked its first centenary as a truly independent and sovereign nation, continues to evolve.

● *Like all northerners, Oslo's citizens make the most of every sunny day*

Culture

Oslo is a thoroughly modern city but one that never loses sight of its traditions. If you came to find people wearing the *bunad*, a traditional costume, you'll have to time your visit to coincide with one of the traditional festivals or a wedding; otherwise, content yourself with viewing these in one of Oslo's many historical museums.

Museums, museums, museums. Oslo loves its museums. Art, architecture, children, literary heroes, skiers, sculptors and painters are just a few of the specialised museums you'll discover in the city. There are also history and folk museums, geological museums, theatre and technology museums, aquariums and ship museums.

Still not enough? Spend some time in an art or zoological museum – Oslo literally has museums from A to Z. These cultural repositories are more than just collections. They are a genuine reflection of the Norwegian history, life and soul. The Viking Ship, Kon-tiki and Fram museum are authentic marvels. These are ships that sailed astonishing distances and made incredible discoveries: not replicas, the real thing. If you intend to sample as many of Oslo's museums as possible, invest in an Oslo Pass (see page 57).

Oslo is also a city of words. Literature has played a strong role in Norwegian culture. Few would dispute the impact and influence of Ibsen, Bjornson or Sigrid Udset. Oslo is still a place that nurtures

● *The Vikings left some ships behind at the Vikingshiphuset museum*

authors. Jostein Gaarder's powerful novel *Sofie's World* has been on the best-selling lists world wide in recent years.

Art, too, is a very powerful influence in everyday Oslo. Art is more than that which is displayed in a contained environment. Art is everywhere in the city, on the streets, along the waterfront and in parks. The sculpture park devoted to the work of Gustav Viegland and the museums devoted to the work of Edvard Munch and other Norwegians artists will sweep you up into the scope and impact of these artists.

Not only is sculpture to be found in the parks of Oslo, there is also music. During the summer months concerts are held in venues all around the city. In winter the music moves indoors to the concert halls and opera house. The contemporary music scene in the city has greatly diversified in recent years. Young and talented musicians are beginning to receive national and international acclaim. One hip music magazine has even taken to referring to 'the Oslo sound', a mix of jazz and electronica. Much of this expansion can be attributed to the spread of clubs, bars and new concert venues that enable both the musicians to express them and for the public to hear them.

Culture is also found in the architecture of the city. Contemporary additions such as the controversial Rådhuset (City Hall) find a comfortable place alongside the neo-classical lines of the Royal Palace. Elsewhere in Oslo you'll find chunks of living history and architecture combined in places like the old quarter in Gamlebyen, filled with centuries-old houses, well preserved and still occupied. It's a city filled with works from both the past and the present, while leaving plenty of room for tomorrow's additions.

▶ *Aker Brygge, the reclaimed harbour area, bustles with life*

MAKING THE MOST OF
Oslo

Shopping

SHOPS

You can shop till you drop in Oslo and there will still be more to buy!
Oslo simply has it all – department stores, small boutiques and
shops, antique emporiums, flea markets, open markets and oodles
of handicraft and souvenir shops. Most shops are open Monday to
Friday 09.00–17.00 and Saturday until 15.00. Department stores are
more generous, keeping open until 20.00 on Friday and 18.00 on
Saturday. Only during the holiday season will you find stores open
on Sundays.

WHAT TO BUY

Traditional Norwegian souvenir shopping would have to include a
brightly coloured, hand-knit *lusehofte* sweater, mittens, gloves or a
scarf. Knitting is a time-honoured tradition in Norway and at school
both boys and girls are taught this art. You might want to take a tip
from Queen Sonja and present your friends with Norwegian pewter
pieces – beer mugs, dishes and bowls are frequently decorated with
traditional designs. For the child on your list you'll find lots of small
cuddly items such as stuffed polar bears, furry seals and even some
Norwegian trolls.

WHERE TO SHOP

If you like your shopping compact start in the city centre area near
Karl Johans Gate. This pedestrian precinct is filled with familiar
chain stores such as Benetton and H&M. Do you prefer one-stop
shopping in a department store or mall? The city centre area is
home to Steen & Strom, Paleet, Glassmagasinet and Byporten.
Grünerløkka (see page 84) is a young and extremely hip area. Small

---

USEFUL SHOPPING PHRASES

What time do they open/close?
Når åpner/stinger den?
Nor orpner/stehng-er dehn?

How much is it?
Hvor mye kostet det?
Vor mew-yer koster deh?

I'd like to buy ...
Jeg kan få ...
Yeh kern for ...

---

independent stores are filled with clothes, pottery, handicrafts and even some used book and record stores. A lot of young Norwegian designers frequently launch their wares in the shops here.

In Majorstua (see page 100) the streets of Bogstadveien and Hegdehaugsveien are a divine mix of both exclusive and mid-price stores. You could spend an entire day exploring these two streets – if your credit card would hold up that long. Bygdøy Allé in Frogner (see page 100) is home to a good selection of modern interior design shops. You may not have gone to Oslo to think about home improvement, but you're sure to find some delicious object that would look just perfect at home. Aside from the design elements there is everything from exclusive underwear to kitchen utensils. This area could give a whole new meaning to the words home improvement. Grønland (see page 84), like Grünerløkka, almost defies description. The markets here are filled with vegetables and ethnic foods and the shops carry everything from fabrics to gold. Take some time to wander the streets of Grønlandsieret and Smalgangen.

Eating & drinking

WHERE TO GO

Traditional Norwegian food comes mostly from the sea. Salmon (*laks*), either grilled, smoked or marinated, is very popular, as is boiled shrimp (*reker*), herring (*sild*), and cod (*torsk*). Boiled potatoes and other vegetables are normally served with the meat or fish. You can expect to see pickled herring and a sweet brown goats cheese (*geitost*) on the breakfast buffets along with the breads and cereals. A favorite Norwegian dessert is cloudberry jam (*moltebaer syltetoy*), served warm with ice cream. Apple cake (*eplekake*) with fresh cream is also popular.

By most standards, Norwegian food is rather bland, and often heavy, although Oslo has some very good restaurants that rate five Michelin stars. For something a little different, you can try steaks from reindeer, moose or whale, which are available at some of the more expensive restaurants. Vegetarians and vegans, admittedly, will find Oslo a challenge, as most menus are based on fish and meat.

At the bottom of the food chain are food wagons and street side kiosks, where you can get hot dogs, hamburgers and soft drinks. Next up are the konditoris, or bakeries, where you can get coffee, fresh pastries and sandwiches. Most have a few tables where you

> ### RESTAURANT CATEGORIES
> The following price guide, used throughout the book, indicates the average price per head for a 2–3 course dinner, excluding drinks. Lunch will usually be a little cheaper in each category.
> **K** = 15–50Kr. **KK** = 55–90Kr. **KKK** = 95–140Kr. **KKK+** = Over 140Kr.

can sit to enjoy your food as you watch the street scene. For more substantial meals, try the kafeterias, which serve traditional, simple meals at reasonable prices. At the top are the kafes and restaurants. A wide variety of traditional and international restaurants can be found, but the prices tend to be high.

Oslo is a seafood-lover's paradise

MAKING THE MOST OF OSLO

Tipping is not required, but most people will round up the bill, and even leave a little extra if the service has been good.

If you are in Oslo on a warm summer day, pick up some sandwiches, desserts and drinks at a konditori and head for Frognerparken or Vigeland Park for a picnic. If you like seafood, you can buy freshly caught and cooked shrimps directly from the fishermen at the harbour. Enjoy shelling and eating them as you stroll along the harbour and buy a beer to wash them down at a local café.

LUTEFISK

The dictionary defines *lutefisk* (pronounced lood-e-fisk) as 'stockfish that has been soaked in lye water, skinned, boned and boiled.' Lye is a strong alkaline liquor containing mainly potassium carbonate, obtained by leaching wood ashes with water. *Lutefisk* is normally served with butter, salt, and pepper. The finished *lutefisk* usually has the consistency of gelatin. Norwegians traditionally serve it for Christmas. It is an acquired taste, and not for the weak of stomach.

The history of the dish dates back to the days of the Vikings. There are many legends surrounding its origin. Most tales involve dried cod that was subsequently caught in a fire. Water was used to put out the fire, and the dried fish was allowed to sit in the slush of the ash and the water. Someone then ate the fish that had been rehydrated with the resulting lye water, and that person apparently liked it. Anyone trying *lutefisk* for the first time would wonder if that person was insane or just very hungry.

The national drink of Norway, if it has one, would be coffee, served strong and black. If you want to dilute the coffee with cream or add sugar you will have to ask for it. On the alcoholic side, most Norwegians consume a rather watery pilsner beer, or aquavit, a very strong and bitter spirit.

There are three types of drinking establishments in Oslo. The high-class bars have modern designs and are frequented by business people in suits. The low-class, or 'brown' bars serve the masses from dusty wooden establishments. The third class is chain or themed bars, such as Irish pubs, aimed mainly at tourists.

USEFUL DINING PHRASES

I would like a table for ... people, please.
Et bord til ..., takk.
Eht boor til ..., terk.

May I see the menu, please?
Kan jeg få menyen, takk?
Kern yeh for men-ew-en, terk?

I am a vegetarian.
Jeg er vegetarianer.
Yeh ar veh-geh-ter-iahner.

Where is the toilet (restroom) please?
Hvor er toalettene, takk?
Voor ar too-er-lehterner, terk?

May I have the bill, please?
Kan jeg få regningen, takk?
Kern yeh for rehg-ning-ehn, terk?

Entertainment & nightlife

First impressions may fool you. Underneath Oslo's outwardly conservative atmosphere beats the heart of a party animal. There are countless cafés, bars and nightclubs to choose from and the atmosphere varies from the ultra-hip to comfortably familiar. Nightlife is an active ingredient of all the various areas of the city. From young and hip Grünerløkka to the more upscale Aker Brygge, or the art-conscious cafés of Majorstua, you'll find plenty to keep you occupied at night. Oslo's nightlife is also very well-dressed. Save your grubby attire for the pub back home. Norwegians expect you to be well shod and stylish. If you are venturing out for a night on the town you'll discover a well dressed crowd.

BARS & CLUBS

What's the difference between a café or a bar and a nightclub? In this city it is sometimes difficult to tell. Many cafés and bars that serve food during the day morph into a nightclub with a DJ playing music around 21.00–22.00 at night. This may also be the time when the cover charge appears. All of the restaurants, bars and nightclubs in Oslo, and all of Norway for that matter, are smoke-free (see page 149), but many have outdoor tables during the summer, and in the winter lots of places provide outdoor heaters to keep their puffing patrons protected from the cold. Most bars and nightclubs are open until the wee small hours of the morning, until about 03.00, at least on Friday and Saturday nights.

MUSIC

Oslo ventures out at night for more than just a tipple. There is a good selection of live stages, concert halls, movies and live theatre.

This is, after all, the home country of Ibsen and Grieg and on almost any given night you'll find it possible to see one of their works being performed. Classical music is very much a part of Oslo's modern nightlife. The city boasts both a fine philharmonic symphony and opera company. You'll have plenty of opportunities to hear Grieg as well as more contemporary composers such as David Monrad Johansen, Geirr Tveitt, Farein Valen and Pauline Hall. If you think there's nothing new in the world of opera, spend a Tuesday or Thursday evening at the Underwater Pub. This is when students

○ *When the sun goes down many cafés are transformed into bars and clubs*

from the State School of Opera try out their skills. And, yes, part of the pub truly is under the sea.

Jazz, fusion and modern folk also have their place in Oslo. Norwegian saxophonist Jan Garbarek is one of the hottest properties on the world music scene: have a listen to some of his work before leaving home and you'll be certain to want to seek his recordings out. The ethereal and haunting music of the Sami people has been experiencing quite a revival and artists such as Aulu Caup and Ils Aslak Valkeapaas are at the top of must see, must listen-to performers. And, yes, you will still find traces of A-Ha, the Norwegian band of the 80s that experienced a few fleeting moments in the world rock spotlight.

Traditional folk dancing and singing is also enjoying something of a renaissance and during the summer months there are plenty of festivals highlighting these activities. A century ago, when Norway was struggling to establish a cultural identity to accompany its newly acquired independence, there was a resurgence in traditional dances such as the polkas, reinlenders and mazurkas. In 2005, as Norway celebrated its centenary, there was another wave of nationalism that once again brought these traditions to the forefront. Today, troupes of leikarringer (folk dancers) appear in competition all over the country.

LISTINGS

To find out what is happening where, the *What's On in Oslo* brochure produced by the tourist office is a good place to start. *Streetwise*, a free publication for night owls, is another good source. Both of these are available in English.

◗ *Theatre is very popular in Oslo, and always an excuse for dressing up*

Sport & relaxation

Norwegians spend a lot of time outdoors, skiing in the winter and sailing, fishing and hiking in the summer. Most activities for visitors are linked to the outdoors.

WINTER SPORTS

Skiing, skiing, skiing, Norway is the home of skiing. Rock carvings four thousand years old show ancient Norwegians on skis. At the 2002 Olympics Norway took 11 gold medals. All forms of skiing are popular in Norway – cross-country, downhill, jumping.

In the second week of March, Oslo hosts the Holmenkollen Ski Festival, which attracts skiers and ski jumpers from around the world, and in the last week of March, Oslo hosts the World Cup Biathlon (see page 9). Ticket prices to the Ski Festival vary from 100Kr. to 300Kr. per day, depending on how good a seat you want.
Tickets Available at Norwegian post offices, by calling ❶ 815 33 133 or on ⓦ www.billettservice.no

⬤ *Winter is the major sports season in Norway*

If you want to do it yourself, there are thousands of kilometres of ski trails in and around Oslo, as well as many alpine runs. In the summer, try the ski-simulator at Holmenkollen. Other winter activities open to the visitor include ice skating and dog sledding

OTHER SPECTATOR SPORTS

Football is also an important sport in Norway, with some 1800 football clubs around the country. Oslo hosts the Norway Cup, the world's largest international football tournament for 9–18s, during the first week of August. Over 1500 teams enter the competition.
Ⓦ www.norway-cup.no/uk

Do you want to play the ponies? Ovrevoll racetrack is just to the west of Oslo at Vollsveien 132. Horse racing starts in April, and runs until December. There is also the Bjerke Trotting track, at Trondheimsveien, with racing Wednesday evenings.
Racing Ⓦ www.ovrevoll.no
Trotting Ⓦ www.bjerke.no

PARTICIPATION SPORTS & ACTIVITIES

Golf is popular in Norway, with several good courses in and around Oslo. For the less energetic, there are also several mini-golf courses.

If you feel a Viking urge and want to ford the fjords, all manner of boats, from yachts to canoes and sea kayaks are available for rent. Just remember that plundering and pillaging are no longer allowed.
Yacht rental Ⓦ www. norwayyachtcharter.com
Canoes & kayaks Ⓦ www.summeroslo.com

For the fitness freaks, most major hotels have swimming pools, saunas and exercise/fitness rooms. There are also public swimming pools and commercial spas and fitness clubs in Oslo.

Accommodation

Oslo cannot be categorised as a budget location; however, it delivers solid value for the pounds or dollars you will spend. Within Oslo you will find accommodation as diverse as the country itself. Be it hostel or chic hotel, you will be able to find your comfort level in Oslo.

HOTELS

Thon Hotel Munch K A basic hotel, reasonably priced and in a central location that can be surprisingly quiet. Rooms have TV, mini-bars and showers. Some rooms are accessible for visitors with mobility problems. The hotel does not have a restaurant.
ⓐ Munchsgate 5. ⓣ 23 21 96 00. ⓦ www.thonhotels.no/munch

City Hotel KK Occupying several floors above a city building, this is an intimate, simple hotel with a very quiet atmosphere. Non-smoking rooms are available. ⓐ Skippergarten 19.
ⓣ 22 41 36 10. ⓦ www.cityhotel.no

Linne Hotel KK A modern business and conference hotel located only 10 minutes by car or T-bane from downtown Oslo. Rooms include cable TV, and a mini-bar. The hotel has a licensed bar and

PRICE RATING
Ratings in this book are based on cost of a double room for one night, not including breakfast (unless otherwise stated).
K = 150–400Kr. **KK** = 400–800Kr. **KKK** = 800–2000Kr.
KKK+ = over 2000Kr.

conference rooms. Free parking and breakfast is included in the room price. ❸ Statsråd Mathiesens vei 12. ❶ 23 17 00 00. Ⓦ www.linne.no

Rica Helsfyr Hotel KK–KKK This modern hotel in a rural location is just a short distance to the T-bane that will take you to most of Oslo's sights. Well equipped and a good deal for those who don't want the hustle and bustle of city life. ❸ Strømsveien 108. ❶ 22 65 70 00. Ⓦ www.rica.no

Best Western Bondeheimen Hotel KKK A traditional hotel that although it has been modernised keeps its Norwegian country soul. Rooms have TV, mini-bar and shower. On site are business facilities and the Kaffistova Restaurant, featuring Norwegian specialties. ❸ Rosenkrantz Gate 8. ❶ 23 21 41 00. Ⓦ www.bondeheimen.com

First Hotel Millenium KKK This newish first-class hotel is right in the heart of Oslo near the Parliament building, Akershus Fortress and Karl Johans Gate. ❸ Tollbugata 25. ❶ 21 02 28 00. Ⓦ www.firsthotels.no

First Hotel Noble House KKK This charming little boutique hotel has an elegant but highly personal ambience. Each unit has a mini-kitchen and some kind of original artwork. Make sure a staff member escorts you to your room, at least the first time, as the maze-like structure of halls may confuse you. ❸ Kongens gate 5. ❶ 23 10 72 00. Ⓦ www.firsthotels.com

Quality Savoy Hotel KKK This is a popular meeting place for travellers and locals alike. Centrally located only two blocks from

Oslo's main street, most things that you will want to see or do are at a convenient distance. Rooms are equipped with telephone, mini-bar, cable TV and hairdryers. Suitable for travellers with disabilities; guide dogs are allowed, at an extra cost. ⓐ Universitesgata 11. ⓣ 23 35 42 00. ⓦ www.choicehotels.no/hotels/no060

Rica Victoria Hotel KKK A first-class business hotel located in the heart of Oslo only a short distance from Aker Brygge, the Parliament and Karl Johans Gate. Amenities include TV, mini-bars, and showers. Breakfast is included. ⓐ Rosenkrantzgate 13 ⓣ 24 14 70 00. ⓦ www.rica.no

Thon Hotel Cecil KKK Located next to the Parliament in the city centre, just a few steps from Karl Johans Gate, the hotel has large, well equipped rooms that include cable TV, air-conditioning, internet, hairdryer and trouser press. Daily breakfast is included in the price. ⓐ Stortingsgata 8. ⓣ 23 31 48 00. ⓦ www.thonhotels.no/cecil

Thon Hotel Europa KKK A casual and informal hotel within easy reach of the city centre. Rooms feature TV, mini-bar and showers. A fitness centre is available. ⓐ St Olavs Gate 31. ⓣ 23 25 63 00. ⓦ www.thonhotels.no/europa

Thon Hotel Opera KKK The hotel is located only a short distance from Oslo Central Station, a real plus for the traveller. The decor is modern and somewhat spartan but the facilities are good and include a fitness centre with sauna, library and coffee shop. The hotel has disability access but guide dogs are only permitted in smoking rooms. Breakfast is included in the room price.

🏠 Christian Frederiks Plass 5. ☎ 24 10 30 30.
🌐 www.thonhotels.no/opera

Thon Hotel Stefan KKK A newish hotel in the city, it is well known for its truly delicious lunch buffet that draws quite a crowd from local businesses. Non-smoking rooms are available. Standard rooms include showers and TV. 🏠 Rosenkrantzgate 1. ☎ 23 31 55 00.
🌐 www.thonhotels.no/stefan

Thon Hotel Terminus KKK In downtown Oslo, the hotel is within easy walking distance of the central railway station. A modern, well equipped hotel, it offers hair-dryer, mini-bar, cable TV and trouser press in the rooms. A daily breakfast is included in the price. The hotel has disability access and guide dogs are allowed at no additional cost. 🏠 Stenersgata 10. ☎ 23 08 02 00.
🌐 www.thonhotels.no/terminus

Thon Hotel Vika Atrium KKK An efficient business-oriented hotel at the edge of the Aker Brygge area, close to transport, shops and restaurants. Rooms feature TV, mini-bars and trouser press.
🏠 Munkedamsveien 45. ☎ 22 83 33 00.
🌐 www.thonhotels.no/vikaatrium

Radisson SAS Plaza Hotel KKK+ The hotel's soaring dramatic exterior of tinted blue glass with a needle summit belies its intimate and well decorated rooms. The views from the upper floors are astonishing. The hotel also features a fitness facility with sauna and swimming pool. 🏠 Sonja Henies Plass 3. ☎ 22 05 80 00.
🌐 www.plaza.oslo.radissonsas.com

Grand Hotel KKK+ The premier hotel in Oslo has been an integral part of the city's daily life since 1874. The distinctive mansard roof and copper tower have been landmarks for decades. Rooms in the 19th-century part of the hotel have all been modernised. Stay where Henrik Ibsen, Henry Ford, Edvard Munch and Dwight Eisenhower have spent a night or two. ⓐ Karl Johans Gate 31 ⓣ 23 21 20 00 ⓦ www.grand.no

HOSTELS

Anker Hostel K This place has a truly international atmosphere and a spit-and-polish approach to cleanliness. Most rooms have at least 4 beds, some have 6. Facilities include laundry, a kitchen and a small bar. ⓐ Storgata 55. ⓣ 22 99 72 00. ⓦ www.ankerhostel.no

Oslo Vandrerhjem IMI K Except in summer this facility is used for student accommodation. Singles and doubles are available, with shared bath. There are laundry and kitchen facilities on site and the location is close to the city centre. ⓐ Haraldsheimvn 4. ⓣ 22 22 29 65. ⓦ www.vandrerhjem.no

YMCA Sleep Inn K This is as basic as a hostel can get. The Sleep Inn only operates during the summer months and fills up quickly. Beds are a mattress on the floor and you'll need to supply your own sleeping bag. But it is a good central choice and kitchen facilities are available. ⓐ Myrerskogveien 54. ⓣ 21 02 36 00. ⓦ www.vandrerhjem.no/osloronningen

▶ *The Grand Hotel presides over the centre of Oslo*

THE BEST OF OSLO

If you have only a limited stay in Oslo, here are ten experiences you shouldn't miss.

TOP 10 ATTRACTIONS

- **Holmenkollen Ski Jump** is Oslo's most frequently visited attraction (see page 100). You can hike to the top to get a breathtaking view of the city, and the course that world class ski-jumpers attempt to conquer.

- **Norwegian Folk Museum** (see page 92). A lovely outdoor museum with the largest collection of cultural history in Norway.

- **Akershus Castle** This centuries-old fortress is still used for state occasions and contains the Resistance Museum, which gives a startlingly forthright account of the German occupation of Norway (see pages 69–70).

- **Kon-tiki Museum** Thor Heyerdahl mesmerised the world with his balsa-log raft voyages across the Pacific Ocean in 1947. The raft, the Kon-tiki, is on permanent display along with artefacts from that voyage and the papyrus boat, the Ra II (see page 94).

- **Viking Ship Museum (Vikingshiphuset)** The Viking ships on display – the Gokstad, Tne and Oseberg, all dating from AD800–900 – are the best-preserved in any museum (see page 92).

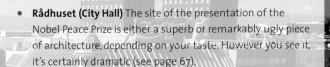

- **Rådhuset (City Hall)** The site of the presentation of the Nobel Peace Prize is either a superb or remarkably ugly piece of architecture, depending on your taste. However you see it, it's certainly dramatic (see page 67).

- **Munch Museet** Edvard Munch's body of work is well represented here along with the works of many other Norwegian artists (see page 84). Although its copy of Munch's most famous painting, *The Scream*, has never been recovered following its theft in 2004, there is still enough here to intrigue even the casual art-lover. (see page 73).

- **Vigeland Sculpture Park** Located in Frogner Park, this is one of Oslo's most remarkable attractions. The 212 dramatic bronze, granite and iron sculptures of Gustav Vigeland depict his vision of humanity in all its forms (see page 102).

- **Children's Art Museum** is for the young and the young-at-heart. This museum is filled with oodles of interactive, hands-on exhibits and a large collection of children's drawings, paintings and handicrafts from around the globe (see page 102).

- **Aker Brygge** Once an active shipyard this abandoned industrial area has been transformed into one of Oslo's most attractive waterfront areas filled with shops and restaurants. It's a perfect place to sip a glass of wine and view the fortress of Akershus across the water (see page 69).

The reclaimed waterfront area attracts citizens and tourists alike

Here's a quick guide to seeing the best of Oslo, depending on the time you have available.

HALF-DAY: OSLO IN A HURRY

If you only have half a day, maybe a spare morning on a business trip, put on your hiking shoes for a walk through the centre that will take you to some of Oslo's top sights. Starting at the main railway station, Oslo S, walk west along Karl Johans Gate towards the Royal Palace (Slottet). The first building on the right is Oslo Domkirke (Cathedral). As you continue along Karl Johans Gate you will come to Stortinget, the home of the Norwegian parliament. Turn left onto Kongens Gate, where you will find the Norwegian Architecture Museum. Turn left again onto Revierstredet where you will see Engebret Café, Oslo's oldest eatery. Turn right onto Kirkegata, and you will pass the newly established Museum of Contemporary Art (entry on Myntgata). At the end of Kirkegata, you will come to a drawbridge which will take you over Kongens Gate

○ *Make time to visit the waterfront attractions of Aker Brygge*

and into Akershus Castle. Work your way north through the fortress and exit through a Gate onto Akersgate. Turn right onto Rådhusgata to see Christiania Torv (Square) and the Theatre Museum. Retrace your steps and continue west on Rådhusgata until you come to the Rådhuset (Town Hall). Walk around the Rådhuset, through Fridtjof Nansens Plass and onto Raold Amundsens Gate, where you will find the National Theatre. Cross Karl Johans Gate and you will be beside the University. Turn left on Kristian IVs Gate which will take you past the National Art Gallery and the History Museum. At Frederiks Gate you can cross into the gardens of the Royal Palace. Work your way south through the Royal Palace complex until you emerge onto Drammensveien and go west. Passing the Ibsen Museum, turn left onto Huitfeldts Gate and left again onto Cort Adelers Gate. This will take you into Aker Brygge. Find a nice restaurant on the waterfront to enjoy lunch and a cold Norwegian beer – you deserve it.

1 DAY: TIME TO SEE A LITTLE MORE

A whole day gives you time to explore one or two of the sights on the half-day walk in more depth. Alternatively, follow the half-day tour in the morning and after lunch take a ferry from Aker Brygge to Bygdøy, getting off at Bygdøynes. As you alight, you will see the Gjoa. Just past the Gjoa is a large plaza, onto which three major maritime museums face: the Fram Museum, the Kon-Tiki Museum, and the Norwegian Maritime Museum. After exploring at least one of these museums, it is worth the extra 1 km (1/2 mile) walk to perhaps the best of them all: follow Bygdøynesveien, turn right onto Langviksveien and left onto Huk Aveny, which will bring you to the entrance of the Viking Ship Museum. From this museum, retrace your steps to Langviksveien. From here, if you still have time, you can

continue north to the Norwegian Folk Museum. From the Folk Museum, continue north on Langviksveien, turn right on Museumsveien, and left onto Huk Aveny. At the end of Huk Aveny, you can catch a ferry back to Aker Brygge and another beer.

2–3 DAYS: SHORT CITY BREAK

The half-day and one-day sightseeing walks can easily be expanded into two or three days if some of the museums take your fancy. But if not, there's still plenty more to pack in. Other sights worth visiting include the Munch Museum, the Holmenkollen Ski Jump, Vigeland Park and Museum, and Gamleyen. Oslo also has many smaller museums dedicated to just about anything you can imagine. Spend at least one evening wining and dining with the locals in Grünerløkka.

LONGER: ENJOYING OSLO TO THE FULL

If you have lots of time, you can easily spend several more days taking in what Oslo has to offer. If you feel a need to get away from the city, however, you can discover Norway outside Oslo. Perhaps the best way is to take the 'Norway in a Nutshell' tour. It can be done in two days (Oslo to Bergen), but you may want to spend up to a week to really get a feel for the country, by adding loops to Stavanger and Sognefjord. Other options include one- or two-day trips down the east coast of Oslofjord to Drobak, Fredrikstad and Halden – by car, bus, train or ferry – or a two- or three-day excursion north to Lillehammer, Roras and Trondheim. Perhaps the best of all for a truly get-away-from-it-all feeling is the coastal cruise north from Bergen. You can go as for north as time and funds allow.

● *The Fram Museum at Bygdøy is well worth a visit*

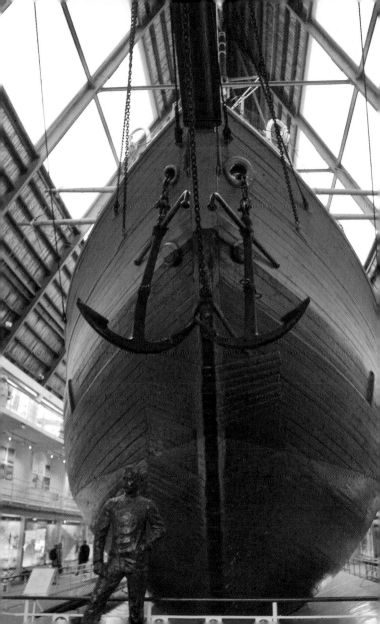

Something for nothing

Oslo would not claim to be the most inexpensive destination in the world, but even in this country of high living standards and matching cost of living there is still plenty for the visitor on a budget to enjoy free of charge. Here are just a few suggestions.

✳ • **Freialand** this chocolate factory tour is free, but watch out for the calories! ❸ Johans Throne Holsts Plass 1. ❶ 22 04 40 22.

✳ • **Astrup Fearnley Museum of Modern Art** is home to an extensive collection of post-war art from Norwegian and many international artists. This privately owned museum opened in 1993. See page 72.

• **Forsvarmuseet** Norway's military history from the Vikings to the 1950s (see page 71). Highlights range from the unions with Denmark and later Sweden to the German invasion and the Battle of the Atlantic during World War II. The museum incorporates dioramas, models and historical objects to recreate this fascinating segment of history.

• **Oslo City Museum** Set in the distinguished Frogner Manor (see page 105), the surroundings themselves are worthy of a visit. The city's thousand-year history is displayed in models, photographs, objects and paintings. The museum also offers historical town walks.

✳ • **Vigeland Park**, Norway's most visited attraction, is filled with more than 200 sculptures by noted artist Gustav Vigeland, who also designed the layout of the park (see page 102).

• **Akebakken Luge Track** if the weather is right (snow on the ground) and you're feeling brave, this popular luge track is open and the admission is free. Even if you don't have your own sled

this is fun to watch. Akebakken, 8 km (5 miles) from the city
centre. Bus 56: Grefsen.

* **Skating** Take a spin on the ice during the winter months at one
  of Oslo's many outdoor rinks. The skating is free, but unless
  you've brought your own blades you'll have to pay to rent skates.
  Most rinks are open every day from December to March.

FREE SURFING IN OSLO
Internet access for free can be found at the Municipal Library,
Deichmanske Bibliotek. You may even book your half hour free
session by calling in advance. Henrik Ibsen Gate.
 23 43 29 00.

Gustav Vigeland's sculpture theme park is an unforgettable sight

When it rains

It's raining? Throw on your best cape and deerstalker hat and head to Æreslunden, Oslo Cathedral's Memorial Graveyard, and contemplate the loss of such notable figures as Edvard Munch and Henrik Ibsen. If you don't want to get wet, then Oslo has a vast range of museums for every taste that will absorb your time. Or follow up some of these other leads:

Baerums Verk (see page 79) is a delightful collection of buildings from 1610 that are filled with craft shops and restaurants. You may have to dodge the raindrops between the buildings but it's a good way to spend a few hours on a dreary day sipping chocolate and admiring the work of artisans. It takes on a festive air at Christmas (see page 12).

When only a mall crawl will satisfy your need to be active but remain dry, head to the city centre for the Byporten Center, next to the Central Station, or Steen & Strom, also in the city centre, an inspired collection of 57 shops offering everything from clothes and books to perfumes, furniture, shoes and toys.

The treasure hunter can justify indoor time in the 1500 square meters of Bislet Second-Hand and Antiques Market (see page 80). There is something for everyone in this attic-like storehouse of goodies: antiques and nearly so, books, crystal and lots of white elephants.

◗ *Oslo gets a lot of rain, but luckily there's plenty to see and do indoors*

On arrival

TIME DIFFERENCES

Oslo's clocks follow Central European Time (CET). During Daylight Saving Time (end Mar–end Oct), the clocks are put ahead 1 hour. In the Norwegian summer, at 12.00 noon, time at home is as follows:

Australia Eastern Standard Time 20.00, Central Standard Time 19.30, Western Standard Time 18.00
New Zealand 22.00
South Africa 12.00
UK and Republic of Ireland 11.00
USA and Canada Newfoundland Time 07.30, Atlantic Canada Time 07.00, Eastern Time 06.00, Central Time 05.00, Mountain Time 04.00, Pacific Time 03.00, Alaska 02.00.

ARRIVING

By air

Oslo International Airport is located at Gardermoen, about 50 km (30 miles) north of the city. Opened in 1998 and still looking very new, with facilities that include banks, ATMs, currency exchange, restaurants, tourist information, newsagents, gift shops and a pharmacy. The airport is usually busy, and the layout requires some long walks, so allow some extra time in planning your schedule on arriving or departing. Be sure to acquire some Norwegian kroner before you leave the airport, as few businesses accept foreign currencies.

From the airport, high-speed trains (Flytoget) go to Oslo S, the central railway station in Oslo. The trains run every 10 minutes, and take about 20 minutes to get there. The fare is 150Kr. There are also express buses to Oslo S operated by SAS Transport Service. The buses leave every 20 minutes, and travel time is about 40 minutes. The fare is 110Kr. one way or 160Kr. return. Taxis are available outside the arrivals area, but the fare to central Oslo is expensive, starting at 600Kr. All major car rental companies rent cars at the airport.

Oslo is served by most international airlines. Domestic flights to other parts of Norway also leave from Gardermoen.

Oslo International Airport ☎ 64 81 20 00. ⓦ www.osl.no
Flytoget ⓦ www.flytoget.no
SAS Transport Service buses ⓦ www.flybussen.no/oslo

Sandefjord Airport Torp is located 110 km (70 miles) south-west of Oslo, and is now Norway's second largest International airport.

IF YOU GET LOST, TRY ...

Excuse me, do you speak English?
Unnskyld meg, snakker du engelsk?
Unshewl mey, snerkur doo ehng-erlsk?

How do I get to ...?
Hvordan kommer jeg til ...?
Voordern kommer yeh til ...?

Can you show me on my map?
Kan du vise meg på kartet?
Kern doo veesur meh po kertur?

Some low-cost airlines are now using this airport as a second gateway to Oslo. The Torp Express bus service connects with arriving flights, and takes about 2 hours to get to the main bus station in Oslo. It is also possible to take a train from Sandefjord to Oslo, but you will need to take a local bus or taxi to the Sandefjord Railway Station. By car, simply take Highway E16 from the airport to Oslo. All the major car hire companies are represented here, too.

Sandefjord Airport Torp Ⓦ www.torp.no

By rail

Oslo Sentralstasjon (Central Station) is simply called Oslo S, and is located at the eastern end of Karl Johans Gate near the centre of the city. Oslo S is the main transportation link in the city. Trains from continental Europe, from other parts of Scandinavia and from other cities in Norway all arrive here, as do the buses and trains from the airports. The main bus station is adjacent to Oslo S and can be reached by an overhead walkway.

Oslo S is well equipped with facilities for the arriving traveller. The Interail centre provides a welcome rest and showers for the weary traveller. There is an efficient tourist information centre that can provide maps, information, and assist with currency exchange, hotel reservations and also sell you an Oslo Card. There is also a post office, an internet café, restaurants and bars inside the station. Taxis, buses, and trams are just outside the station. There is also an underground (T-Banen) station.

The adjacent shopping centre, Byporten, can be accessed directly from the main gallery. On the southern side you will find Østbanehallen, the old part of the station, now converted into a small shopping arcade.

ⓐ Jernbanetorvet1. Ⓦ www.nsb.no Ⓒ Daily 07.00–23.00.

By bus

Bussterminalen, the main bus station (Oslo M) is situated on the north side of Oslo's central railway station, which makes transfers between the two all the easier. All local bus services as well as those arriving from further afield arrive and depart from here.

ⓐ Schweigaards Gate 8.

By ferry

International ferries arrive and depart from two piers. Vippetangen pier is just below Akershus Castle and Hjortneskaia pier is adjacent to Aker Brygge. Both are on the waterfront close to the centre of Oslo.

Ferries to other parts of the Oslo Fjord leave from Vippetangen. Ferries to Bygdøy Peninsula leave from Rådhusbrygge 3 in front of the Rådhus (City Hall). These ferries only run in the warmer months, mid-April to early October.

Driving

Cars must pay a 15 to 25Kr. toll each time they enter Oslo. Oslo has

TRAFIKANTEN

Trafikanten is an information office for public transportation in and around Oslo. It is located next to Oslo S at Jernbanetorget. The office has timetables for trains, buses, trams, the underground (T-Banen), and ferries that operate in Oslo, the greater Oslo area, and Central Eastern Norway.

ⓐ Jernbanetorvet 1 ☎ 81 50 01 76. ⓦ www.trafikanten.no (information in Norwegian only) 🕐 07.00–20.00 Mon-Fri, 08.00-18.00 Sat, Sun.

many one-way streets, which can make driving around confusing, although traffic congestion is not a problem. There is lots of parking in the centre of the city, but it can be expensive. There is metered parking on the streets: expensive during business hours (up to 50Kr. per hour) but normally free during other times. There are also many parking garages, but they can cost up to 200Kr. per day. The Oslo Pass gives free parking in municipal car parks.

FINDING YOUR FEET

Finding your feet in Oslo is easy. This is user-friendly city, and the people are open and generous. Many of the attractions and hotels are close enough to the city centre that they can be reached on foot. Good pubic transportation is available to reach those further out. Crime is not a worry if you take the normal precautions. However, prices and taxes are high in this city, so be prepared to pay for everything from road tolls to pay toilets.

ORIENTATION

Karl Johans Gate is the main street in central Oslo. It runs east–west, with Oslo S at the eastern end and the Royal Palace at the western end. Most hotels, as well as many of the city's attractions, are within a 15-minute walk of Karl Johans Gate. The waterfront, Aker Brygge, Rådhuset and Akershus Castle are just a few blocks south of Karl Johans Gate. Most streets, especially those in central Oslo, follow a standard grid pattern.

GETTING AROUND
Public transport
Getting around the city is quite easy. The centre part of the city is easily and safely walkable, and considering the Norwegians'

penchant for hiking, this is the preferred mode of transport. If you want to travel a little further afield, the public transport system, consisting of buses, trams and T-banc (metro, subway), is very efficient. Tickets for single trips cost 20Kr. if purchased in advance, or 30Kr. if purchased from the driver. Advance tickets can be purchased from 7-eleven stores, Narvesen kiosks, and from Trafikanten. Daily passes cost 55Kr. Multi-day passes are also available. The Oslo Pass gives free transport during the daytime and evening, but not late at night. Note that there is an honour system regarding tickets, and the fine for travelling without a ticket is a hefty 750Kr.

OSLO PASS

If you intend to visit a number of attractions in a short period of time, you should invest in the Oslo Pass. It gives free admission to most museums and attractions, free travel on public transport (except night buses), free parking in municipal car parks, and discounts on sightseeing, car rentals, and reduced prices at some restaurants and amusement parks. The card is available in 24-, 48-, and 72-hour versions, and can be purchased for individual adults and children, or as a family pass (two adults, two children). It can be purchased at Tourist Information Centres, and most major hotels, some Narvesen kiosks, at Trafikanten (see page 53), or through the net, ⓦ www.visitoslo.com. An information booklet outlining all the benefits comes with the Oslo Pass.

An Oslo Package is also available, which includes hotel accommodations as well as the Oslo Pass.

MAJORSTUA

Frognerparken ←

HEGDEHAUGEN

Bogstadveien

Kirkeveien

Holmenkollen,
Internasjonale Barnekunstmuseet,
Bogstad Herregard

12

19

10,17

Hegdehaugsveien

Vigelandsmuseet ←

URANIENBORG

FROGNER

12

19

Slottsparken

Slottet

St Olavs Gate

Frederiksgate

10,17

Kristian IVs G

Universitets Gate

10,13,19

Drammensveien

13

10

Karl Johans

Stortinge

10,12

Munkedamsveien

Fridtjof Nansens
Plass

SKILLEBEKK

13

30

Rådhuset

10,12

FILIPSTAD

AKER BRYGGE

Akers
Slott

Ferry 91 to Bygdøy

N

BYGDØY ←

0   500m

O s l o f j o r d e n

GRÜNERLØKKA

Airport
Gardermoen

Toftesgate

30

11,12

Sarsgate

13,17

FREDENSBORG

Kunstindustriemuseet

Botanical
Garden

Munch
Museum

11,12,13

H. Ibsens Gate

30

Nylandsveien

10,11,17,18

13,19

Oslo Spektrum

Oslo Domkirke

Prinsens Gate

19,12

18,19

GRØNLAND

Oslo S
(central rail station)

dhusgata

18,19

rsvarsmuseet

GAMLEBYEN

∙∙∙∙∙∙∙∙	Ferry
▬▬▬▬	Bus
▬▬▬▬	Tram

Taxis

Taxis are easy to find and use in Oslo. They are safe and clean, but they can be expensive. The fare starts at up to 50Kr. plus up to 20Kr. per kilometre. It is cheaper to flag a taxi rather than to call one, as the flag drops when a called taxi is dispatched and you can owe a small fortune before the taxi picks you up.

CAR HIRE

Rental cars are readily available, and most major rental agencies are represented at both the airport and in Oslo. However, rental car rates are very high, and car insurance is extra. Some local rental agencies offer lower rates, but the cars can be questionable, and they have been known to add extras charges. If you get a traffic ticket, the fine will be automatically charged to the credit card you used to hire the car. Major rental agencies include:

Avis Gardermoen Airport: ❶ 64 81 06 60. Torp: ❶ 33 46 95 50. City: ❸ Munkedamsveien 27. ❶ 81 56 90 44. Ⓦ www.avis.no

Budget Torp: ❶ 33 44 63 33. City: ❸ Munkedamsveien 27. ❶ 81 56 06 00. Ⓦ www.budget.no

Hertz At Gardermoen and Torp airport and City: ❸ Sigrid Undsets Plass. ❶ 64 81 05 50. Torp: ❶ 33 47 15 38. Railway Station: ❸ Jernbanetorget 1. ❶ 22 10 00 00. Ⓦ www.hertz.no

Europcar Gardermoen Airport: ❶ 64 81 05 60. Torp: ❶ 33 46 42 00. City: ❸ Haakon VII Gate 9. ❶ 22 83 12 42. Ⓦ www.europcar.no

Rent-a-Wreck Gardermoen Airport ❶ 63 97 88 11. Torp: ❶ 33 46 87 87. Ⓦ www.rent-a-wreck.no

National Torp: ❶ 33 47 68 00.

---

❶ *Oslo's northern latitude gives it beautiful sunsets*

Central Oslo

The centre of Oslo is a hive of activity. You'll find restaurants, shops, bars, cafés and discos all within reasonable distance of Karl Johans Gate. Everybody comes to this area – old, young, wealthy or on a student budget – there's something for everyone. Karl Johans is where you will find most of the shops and restaurants. Head to Rosenkrantz Gate for dance clubs and discos. Are you in the mood for jazz? You'll find most of the blues and jazz clubs near Stortovet. Something classical? The concert and opera halls are within walking distance of Karl Johans Gate.

SIGHTS & ATTRACTIONS

Karl Johans Gate

Located in the very heart of Oslo is the best known and liveliest street in the city, if not the entire country. Named after King Karl Johans, the street was designed by architect H.D.F. Linstow in 1840. Here is where you will find many of Norway's premier institutions, such as Slottet (the Royal Palace), Stortinget (the Norwegian Parliament) and the National Theatre. Karl Johans, as it is usually known, is one of the best places to shop till you drop and then have a bite to eat. In the winter, the upper part of Karl Johans is transformed into a skating rink.

Slottet – Det Kongelige Slot (Royal Palace)

Located at the very head of Karl Johans Gate, this royal residence creates an imposing focal point. It was commissioned by King Karl Johan of Sweden (see feature box on page 66) following his ascent

● *The royal palace is impressive, but not a great place to live*

Teater

ortinget

Grensen

Stortorvet

Oslo Domkirke

H. Ibsens Gate

Norske
Opera

Oslo City

Jernbanetorget

Byporten

Oslo S
(central rail station)

Nylandsveien

Kongens gate

Prinsens Gate

Kirkegata

Christiania
Torv

Postmuseet

ankplassen

Rådhusgata

Museet for
Samtidskunst

Grev Wedels
Plass

Astrup Fearnley
Museum

Gamle Logen

Akershusstranda

Forsvarsmuseet

KARL JOHAN

The King of Sweden (and Norway) known to the Scandinavians as Karl Johan is better known to the rest of the world as Jean Bernadotte. Born of humble origins in rural France, he rose to power as one of Napoleon's marshals – and the Emperor's brother-in-law. When he was offered the crown of Sweden after the disastrous French retreat from Moscow he promptly accepted it and then led the Swedish army against his former master. A born survivor, he was the only member of Napoleon's court to establish a royal dynasty.

to the throne in 1818, after Norway had been ceded by Denmark to Sweden. The king was keen to emphasise his claim to rule Norway as well as Sweden, and commissioning this palace was an important aspect of his PR campaign. Work on the elaborate neo-classical structure began in 1825 but it overran its budget by several times; it was not completed until 1848, by which time the king had died. In fact the palace was seldom used by the Swedish monarchs and often shut up in darkness; when the first King of Norway, Haakon, took over the palace in 1905 it was considered uninhabitable (no running water or WCs, for instance) and Haakon was reluctant to burden the state with the expense of renovation. It wasn't until as recently as 1991, on King Harald's accession, that a full evaluation was carried out and the decay was even worse than feared; the restoration costs are still controversial and work has only been partly carried out. However, some state rooms have been fully and magnificently renovated and are open to the public.

Tours of the interior are restricted, but normally available in summer: call for more information. The gardens surrounding the palace are always open to the public. There is a changing of the guard every day at 13:30.

ⓐ Drammensveien 1. ❶ 22 04 87 00. ⓦ www.kongehuset.no
🕒 Generally 11.00–18.00 late Jun–mid-Aug. ⓝ T-bane: Nationaltheateret

Stortinget (Parliament Building)

Norway's National Assembly building was built in the 1860s of yellow brick and reddish granite. The assembly chamber, which seats the 165 members of the parliament, was designed to resemble an amphitheatre. The building has been richly embellished, both inside and out, by various Norwegian artists, including a tapestry, *Solens Gang*, by artist Karen Holtsmark. Guided tours are bookable on direct application.

ⓐ Karl Johans Gate 22. ❶ 23 31 31 80.
ⓦ www.stortinget.no/english/index.html ⓝ T-bane: Stortinget.

Rådhuset (City Hall)

Rådhuset is best known as the location from which the Nobel Peace Prize is awarded each year in December. Oslo's City Hall, designed by Arnstein Arneberg and Magnus Poulsson, is a splendid example of modernist architecture. However, after the building opened in 1950 it took the residents of the city a long time to warm to its radical departure from classical design. The ceremonial main hall of the complex covers 1519 sq m (16,350 sq ft) of space and is graced by Henrik Sorenson's oil painting, the largest in Europe, on the rear wall.

ⓐ Fridtjof Nansens Plass. ❶ 23 46 16 00.
ⓦ www.rft.oslo.kommune.no 🕒 Mon–Fri 08.30–16.00, Sat & Sun 12.00–16.00. ⓝ Tram 10, 12 or 15: Rådhusplassen.

◯ *Not everyone liked the City Hall's stark, modern lines when it was built*

Christiania Torv

This was Oslo's original market square, renamed with the old city name in 1958. In the 1990s the square was made vehicle-free when a tunnel was created to divert traffic. Now this very pleasant area of the city is surrounded by historic buildings and filled with outdoor cafés.

ⓐ Kvadraturen. ◯ Tram 10 or 12: Christiania Torv

Aker Brygge

Once an active shipyard, this large chunk of Oslo's downtown waterfront has now been transformed into a trendy shopping and entertainment area. Many travellers will tell you that this is one of the most attractive places in Europe, the Oslo equivalent of San Francisco's Fisherman's Wharf. It's a delightful destination from which to enjoy a glass of wine or a truly fabulous dinner while taking in a panoramic view of the Akershus fortress across the water. You can find a range eating places but the largest selection is available to those with well padded wallets. But it won't cost you a Krone to wander the waterfront.

🅐 Bryggigatai 9. 🆃 22 83 26 80. Ⓝ T-bane: Nationaltheateret; Bus 21, 30, 31, 33, 54 or 71: Aker Brygge; Tram 10 or 12: Aker Brygge.

Akershus Slott & Festning (Akershus Castle & Fortress)

This is probably the most striking sight in Oslo. King Haakon V ordered the start of construction of the fortress to protect the city after he declared Oslo the capital of Norway in 1299. Over the years the structure has been subject to attacks, fires, expansions, improvements and renovations. It is still under the control of the military, and may be closed at any time for military or state functions.

The fortress is strategically located on the eastern shore of the harbour, from which point it dominates the entire harbour. Gun towers were added in 1559, and for the next 200 years it was further fortified with moats and ramparts. From 1637 to 1648 it was developed into a Renaissance royal residence, and most of the luxurious state rooms, mausoleums and chapels date to this time. The crypts of Kings Haakon VII and Olaf V lie beneath the main chapel. By the early 19th century, the requirement for defence was relaxed, and many of the ramparts were removed to make room for public space.

Akershus became infamous during World War II, when the Nazis took control of Norway, and used it as a headquarters and as a site to execute many Norwegian patriots. The Resistance Museum, which is part of the complex, graphically describes the German occupation and the Norwegian resistance movement.

Today Akershus is one of Oslo's top tourist attractions. Besides the lavish state rooms and chapels, the dungeons are interesting to see. There is an information centre just inside the main entrance gate, and guided tours are available. There is also a changing of the guard every day at 13.30.

🅐 Akersgata. ☎ 23 09 39 17. 🅦 www.mil.no/felles/ak/start/museer/
🕓 Mon–Sat 10.00–16.00, Sun 12.30–16.00, May–Sept.
🚋 Tram 10 or 12: Christiania Torv.

Norges Hjemmefrontmuseum (Norwegian Resistance Museum)
Housed in one of the old buildings of the Akershus fortress complex, near the memorial on the spot where Norwegian patriots were executed by the Germans during World War II, this museum was created through the initiative of people who had been actively engaged in the Norwegian Resistance. Five years of occupation from invasion to liberation are uncompromisingly recreated through documents, posters, artefacts and original newspapers and sound recordings.

🅐 Building 21, Akershus Festning. ☎ 23 09 31 38.
🅦 www.mil.no/felles/nhm/start/eng/ 🕓 Mon–Sat 10.00–16.00, Sun 11.00–16.00 15 Apr– 14 Jun & Sept; Mon, Wed, Fri & Sat 10.00–17.00, Tues & Thurs 10.00–18.00, Sun 11.00–17.00, 15 June– 31 Aug; Mon–Sat 10.00–15.00, Sun 11.00–16.00 1 Oct–14 Apr.

Forsvarsmuseet

Another part of the Akershus complex is devoted to Norway's military history from the Vikings to the 1950s. Highlights include the union with Denmark and later Sweden, the German invasion and the Battle of the Atlantic during World War II. The museum incorporates dioramas, models and historical objects to recreate this fascinating segment of history.

Nedre Akershus Festning. 23 09 35 82.
www.mil.no/felles/fmu/start/museet/English/ Tues–Fri 11.00–16.00, Sat & Sun 10.00–17.00, 1 Sept–30 Apr; Mon–Fri 10.00–17.00, Sat & Sun 11.00–17.00, 1 May–31 Aug. Admission free.
Tram 10 or12: Christiania Torv; Bus 60: Myntgata.

Den Gamle Logen

This is a building with a story to tell. Many stories. It was here that Vidkun Quisling was sentenced to death for treason at the close of World War II. At various times this building has served as a place for city council meetings, a concert hall and labour office. Finally in 1980 the Oslo Summer Opera moved in and once again the building is being used for musical events.

Grev Wedels Plass 2. 22 33 44 70.
www.logen.no/english/index.html Tram 10 or 12: Christiania Torv.

Oslo Domkirke (Cathedral)

This beautifully ornate church dating from 1699 is the principal church for the diocese of Oslo. Over the years the church has undergone many renovations and the various fashions of the centuries are reflected in many of the decorative aspects. Among some of the prominent adornments is a stained glass window by artist Emmanuel Vigeland (brother of sculptor Gustav Vigeland), a silver sculpture of the Lord's

Supper by Arrigo Minerib and bronze doors by Dagfin Werenskiold. The marvellous painted ceiling was created by Hugo Louis Mohr between 1936 and 1950. The church has played and continues to play a prominent role in the city. In 2001 the wedding ceremony of Prince Haakon and Mette-Marit took place here.

ⓐ Stortorvet. ⓣ 23 31 46 00. ⓦ www.oslodomkirke.no ⓛ Daily 10.00–16.00. Ⓝ Bus 37: Stortorvet

Universitetet

Oslo University dominates the north-east side of Karl Johans Gate. The three buildings of the complex are built in the neo-classical style and together with the National Theatre create an imposing atmosphere. The Aula, an auditorium built in 1911, houses several murals by Edvard Munch. Munch considered these paintings to be his masterpiece. Until the Rådhuset was built the Nobel Peace Prize was presented in the Aula.

ⓐ Karl Johans Gate. ⓣ 22 85 50 50. ⓦ www.uio.no/english
Ⓝ T-bane: Sognsvann or Storo; Tram 10 or 17.

CULTURE

Astrup Fearnley Museum of Modern Art

Home to an extensive collection of post-war art from Norwegian and many international artists, this privately owned museum opened in 1993.

ⓐ Dronningensgate 4. ⓣ 22 93 60 60. ⓦ www.af-moma.no
ⓛ Tues–Fri 11.00–17.00, Thur 11.00–19.00, Sat & Sun 12.00–17.00. Admission free. Ⓝ Tram 10, 12 or 19: Tollbugata/Dronningensgate. Bus: 30, 31, 32, 54, 60 or 81b: Dronningensgate/Kongensgate. T-bane: Stortinget or Jernbanetorget.

Nasjonalgalleriet (National Gallery)

This is home to Norway's largest public collection of paintings, sculptures, drawings, engravings and many other forms of art. The Edvard Munch Hall contains a number of the artist's most famous works, including the only surviving painted version of *Shrik* (*The Scream*), the most famous of the artist's work. (The other painting was stolen from the Munch Museum in 2004 and has never been recovered; Munch reproduced the painting in other media, too.) The museum also features the work of other Norwegian artists and foreign mansters, including Christian Krohg, El Greco, Modigliani, Peter Balke and Harald Sohlberg.

Ⓐ Kristian Augusts Gate 23. ☎ 21 98 20 00.
Ⓦ www.nationalmuseum.no 🕐 Tues–Wed, 10.00–18.00, Thur 10.00–20.00, Fri 10.00–18.00, Sat & Sun 10.00–17.00. Ⓣ T-bane: Nationaltheatret. Tram 10, 11, 17, 18: Tullinløkka. Tram 13, 19 and bus: Nationaltheatret.

Historisk Museum (Historical Museum)

This is a collection of the three university museums, Oldsaksamlingen (National Antiquities Collection), Etnografisk Museum (Ethnographic Museum), and Mynkabinettet (Collection of Coins and Medals). Together they thoroughly document Norwegian history from the earliest settlements to the present.

Ⓐ Frederiks Gate 2 ☎ 22 85 99 12. Ⓦ www.khm.uio.no/english
🕐 Tues–Sun 11.00–16.00 15 Sept–14 May; Tues–Sun 10.00–16.00 15 May–14 Sept. Ⓣ T-bane: Nationaltheateret.

Stenersenmuseet (Sternersen Museum)

The museum is named after author and art collector Rolf Stenersen, who in 1936 donated his entire collection to the city of Oslo. It was not until 1994 that the collection was removed from storage and placed in this new museum, along with the private collections of Amaldus Neilsen and Ludvig Ravensberg, two of Norway's more prominent artists of the 19th century. The collection includes paintings and drawings by Edvard Munch, a close friend of Stenersen, Kai Fjell and Jakob Weiderman.

@ Munkedamsveien 15. @ 23 49 36 00.

@ www.stenersen.museum.no @ Wed, Sat & Sun 11.00–17.00, Tues & Thur 11.00–19.00. @ T-bane: Nationaltheatret.

Nationaltheatret (National Theatre)

The theatre opened its doors in 1899 with a production of Ibsen's *An Enemy of the People* and since that time has consistently kept the playwright's work at the core of its repertoire. You'll get more than just a night at the theatre when you purchase a ticket to one of the productions: the building houses one of the country's finest art collections, with works by Vigeland, Werenskold, Fjell and Krohg. The baroque-style building was designed by Henrik Bull and is typical of theatre architecture in Europe of the late 19th century.

@ Johansne Dybwads Plass 1, off Stortingsgate. @ 81 50 08 11.

@ www.nationaltheatret.no

@ T-bane: Nationaltheatret; Tram: 12, 13 or 19.

Det Norske Teatret (Theatre of Norway)

This opened in 1913 but never had a permanent home until 1995, when the curtain went up on this ultra-modern construction. This is the main venue in Oslo for works in Norwegian, both classical and modern.

@ Kristian IVs Gate 8. @ 22 42 43 44. @ www.detnorsketeatret.no

⬢ *Konserthus is the Oslo Philharmonic's home base*

Oslo Konserthus (Oslo Concert Hall)

Opened in 1977, this is home to the Oslo Philharmonic Orchestra and is the leading venue for concerts and musical productions in the city. More than 300 events are staged here annually and the hall plays an important role in the cultural life of Oslo. The building was specially designed to present orchestral works and the podium is large enough to accommodate 120 musicians at a single time.

ⓐ Munkedamsveien 14. ❶ 23 11 31 00. Ⓦ www.oslokonserthus.no
Ⓝ T-bane: Nationaltheatret.

Oslo Nye Teater (New Theatre)

This is the home of some of Oslo's more urbane and modern theatre presentations. For many years the repertoire was dominated by comedy but in recent years the emphasis has shifted to greater diversity. Productions are staged in three locations: Rosenkrantz Gate, the Centralteateret in Akersgata and the Dukketeartet (puppet theatre) in Frognerparken.

ⓐ Rosenkrantz Gate 10. ☎ 22 34 86 00.
ⓦ www.oslonye.no/kontakt_oss Ⓣ T-bane: Stortinget.

Den Norske Opera (Norwegian State Opera)

It wasn't until 1959 that Oslo acquired its first opera house, built on the premises of the Folketeatret. Unfortunately this building does not have the ideal acoustics for operatic performances but it won't be until 2010 that a new opera house will open.

ⓐ Storgata 23. ☎ 81 54 44 88. ⓦ www.operaen.no
Ⓣ T-bane: Nygata/Storgata.

Norsk Arkitekture Museet (Norwegian Museum of Architecture)

In March 2005 this museum closed its exhibition space at Kongens Gate 4. In the spring 2007 new premises will be opened in the former Bank of Norway building in Oslo at Bankplassen 3. The Norwegian architect, Sverre Fehn, will be responsible for the reconstruction of the old building and an exhibition pavilion will be built in the garden.

ⓐ Postboks 7014, St. Olavs Plass. ☎ 21 98 20 00.

Teatermuseet (Theatre Museum)

The Theatre Museum is housed in the building that was once the town hall when Oslo was called Christiana. The collection of exhibits outlines the history of theatre in Oslo from 1800. This is a two-for-one experience, as the old town hall is an interesting building in itself.

🅰 Rådhusplassen. ☎ 22 42 65 09.

🅦 www.teatermuseet.no/english.html 🕐 Wed 11.00–15.00, Thur & Sun 12.00–16.00. 🚊 Tram 10, 12 or 15: Rådhusplassen.

Museet for Samtidskunst

This museum contains Norway's largest collection of Norwegian and international art of the post-war period. The permanent collection is so large that only a part of it is on display at any one time. Famous works include Gunnar Gundersen's *Winter Sun* and some of Per Manning's photographic portraits of animals.

The art nouveau building that houses the collection makes an interesting contrast to the contemporary art adorning its exhibit halls.

🅰 St. Olavs Gate 1. ☎ 22 03 65 40.

🅦 www.nationalmuseum.no/index.php/content/view/full/1530

🕐 Tues–Wed & Fri 11.00–17.00, Thur 11.00–20.00, Sat & Sun 12.00–16.00. 🚌 Bus 46, 37 or 33: Nordahl Bruns Gate. T-bane: Nationaltheatret.

Postmuseet (Postal Museum)

With email and mobile phones at our fingertips it's difficult to remember that all important communications once rested in the hands of the post office; this museum brings back those days. There is, of course, an extensive collection of stamps (including some with printing errors), uniforms and even weapons.

🅰 Kirkegata 20. ☎ 23 14 81 62. 🅦 www.norwaypost.no

🕐 Mon–Fri 10.00–17.00, Sat 10.00–14.00, Sun 12.00–16.00.

RETAIL THERAPY

The city centre area around Karl Johans Gate is pedestrian-friendly and packed with shopping malls and department stores. You won't have any problem finding a souvenir or a special treat for yourself.

Shopping malls

Paleet You can come here to shop in this weatherproof complex of some 45 stores, or simply to admire the bronze statue of Norwegian skating heroine Sonja Henje. Most of the shops inside Paleet are fairly upmarket. ⓐ Karl Johans Gate 37–43. ❶ 22 03 38 88.
Ⓦ www.paleet.no Ⓛ Mon–Fri 10.00–20.00, Sat 10.00–18.00.
Ⓝ T-bane: Nationalteatret.

Byporten Adjacent to Central Station, this mega-mall has more than 70 stores. There are also cafés, restaurants and bars mingled among the toy, sport and fashion sellers. The Scandic Hotel forms part of this complex. ⓐ Jernbanetorget 9. ❶ 23 36 20 11.
Ⓦ www.byporten.no Ⓛ Mon–Fri 10.00–21.00, Sat 10.00–18.00.
Ⓝ Tram: Jernbanetorget/Oslo S.

Oslo City Also close to Central Station, with lots of fashion, book and department stores. ⓐ Stenersgata 1. ❶ 81 54 40 33.
Ⓦ www.oslocity.no Ⓛ Mon–Thur 10.00–18.00, Fri 09.00 –18.00, Sat 09.00–15.00. Ⓝ T-bane: Jernbanetorget.

Stores and smaller shops

Glasmagsinet One of the bigger department stores in Norway, it's an excellent place to search out something special for your home. Among other things, this store is the largest outlet for Hadeland

Glassverk, prime Norwegian glassware. You'll also find an excellent coffee shop and restaurant for when that sinking feeling from too much shopping overcomes you. ❸ Stortorvet 9. ❶ 22 90 87 00. Ⓦ www.glasmagasinet.no Ⓝ Bus 37 or 46.

Bare Jazz A treasure trove for jazz lovers located in Oslo City Centre. ❸ Grensen 8. ❶ 22 33 20 80. Ⓦ www.barejazz.no ❺ Mon–Wed 10.00–22.00, Thur–Sat 10.00–24.00.

Norway Designs Clothes, jewellery, paper, if it has a Norwegian twist you will find it here. ❸ Stortingsgaten 28. ❶ 23 11 45 10. Ⓦ www.norwaydesigns.no ❺ Mon–Fri 09.00–17.00, Thur 09.00–19.00, Sat 10.00–15.00.

Logo Shoes for the young and trendy. Don't forget this is Norway and how well you dress your feet is a very Norwegian thing. ❸ Kristian Augusts Gate 5. ❶ 22 20 03 01. ❺ Mon–Fri 10.00–18.00, Thur 10.00–19.00, Sat 10.00–16.00. Ⓝ Tram 10, 11 or 17.

Smykketeatret Just the place to find an original piece of jewellery by a Norwegian artist. In addition you'll also find hand-crafted pieces from Indonesia, designer jewellery from Denmark, steel work from Germany and gold from Israel. ❸ Kristian Augusts Gate 3. ❶ 21 53 12 22. Ⓦ www.smykketeatret.no

Handelsstedet Baerums Verk Set in an ironworks that dates from 1610 this market is one of the more special shopping places in Oslo for unique handicrafts. If you get tired of shopping there is always the museum for a wander. ❸ Verksgata 1. ❶ 67 13 00 18. Ⓦ www.baerumsverk.no ❺ Mon–Fri 10.00–20.00, Sat 10.00–18.00.

Bislet Antiques & Second Hand Market The treasure hunter will love the 1500 sq m (14,400 sq ft) of everything: books, household goods, china, crystal and the odd antique. Great fun for a rainy day.
🅐 Theresesgate 35b. ☎ 22 60 12 33. 🆆 www.bisletantikvariat.no
🕐 Mon–Fri 11.00–17.00, Thur 11.00–18.00 Sat 11.00–15.00.

TAKING A BREAK

Foxx Trendy little coffee bar in the Hotel Continental, conveniently right next door to the National Theatre. 🅐 Stortingsgata 24–26.
☎ 22 82 41 74. 🆆 www.hotel-continental.no 🕐 Mon–Fri 07.30–24.00, Sat 07.30–01.00, Sun 12.00–24.00.

Hambro's Café & Confectioners One of the classiest coffee shops in the city. Subtle colours and antique furnishings whisk you away to a bygone era. All sorts of goodies from the bakery, including filled ciabattas and luscious pastries. 🅐 Kristian IVs Gate 7. ☎ 22 82 60 00.
🆆 www.bristol.no 🕐 Mon–Fri 11.00–20.00, Sat 11.30–18.00.

Grand Café It is said that Ibsen ate his lunch at this café every day. A little pricey, but worth it for the atmosphere and the cake buffet.
🅐 Karl Johans Gate 31. ☎ 23 21 20 18. 🆆 www.grand.no . 🕐 Mon–Tues 11.00–23.00, Wed–Sat 11.00–00.30, Sun 12.00–23.00.

AFTER DARK

Restaurants
TGI Friday KK Yes, it's an American chain restaurant with predictable

▶ *Follow Munch's example and dine at the Theatercaféen*

choices of ribs and steaks on the menu, but it's affordable and lively.
ⓐ Karl Johans Gate 35. ❶ 22 33 32 00.

Enzo Bar and Restaurant KKK A touch of the Mediterranean at the
Radisson Hotel. A good place to start with a drink or stay for dinner.
ⓐ Holbergs Gate 30 ❶ 23 29 30 00 Ⓦ www.radisson.com

Lofoten Fiskerestaurant KKK The perfect choice for a summer eve in
Oslo. You can sit either inside or out and enjoy perhaps the most
delectable fish in the city. The décor is modern and stylish, like so
much of the area in Aker Brygge. The menu changes several times
during the year to take full advantage of each season's specialities.
ⓐ Stranden 75. ❶ 22 83 08 08. Ⓦ www.lofotenfiskerestaurant.com.
🕐 Mon–Sat 11.00–01.00, Sun 12.00–24.00.

Theatercaféen KKK This restaurant opened in 1901 and retains an
authentic turn-of-the-century sumptuousness and flair that is
distinctly its own. It has been a haven for many of Norway's
notables, including Edvard Munch, Knut Hamsun and Johansen.
ⓐ Stortingsgaten 24–26. ❶ 22 82 40 50. 🕐 Mon–Sat 11.00–23.00, Sun
15.00–22.00.

Bars & clubs
34 Sky Bar Will it be the breathtaking views or the designer martinis
that you remember the most? Also worth stopping by during the
day for their tapas lunch. ⓐ Sonja Henies Plass 3. ❶ 22 05 80 34.
Ⓦ www.34etg.no 🕐 Mon–Thur 16.00–01.00, Fri–Sat 16.00–02.00.

Etoile Bar Set above the city on the 7th floor of the Grand Hotel, this
charming bar is lovely place at which to top off an evening out in

the city. ➋ Karl Johans Gate 31 ➊ 23 21 20 00. Ⓦ www.grand.no
🕐 Mon–Thur 11.00–24.00, Fri–Sat 11.00–01.00.

Macondo Currently one of the hottest spots in Oslo. It's 70s-inspired interior is a retro trip. Expect long queues, so don't go on a cold winter night. ➋ Badstugata 1. ➊ 22 20 82 55 .
Ⓦ www.nattguiden.no/utested/583 c Mon–Thur 16.00–01.00, Fri & Sat 16.00–02.00.

Onkel Donald One of Oslo's hotspots, this café-bar combines really good Norwegian food with a chic atmosphere. Late at night it changes from an eatery to a late night bar. ➋ Universitetsgaten 26. ➊ 23 35 63 10. Ⓦ www.onkeldonald.no 🕐 Mon–Tues 11.00–01.00, Wed–Sat 11.00–03.00, Sun 12.00–01.00.

Sikamikanico DJs of all types set an ever-changing tone at one of the city's best club scenes. ➋ Møllergata 2. ➊ 22 41 44 09.
Ⓦ www.sikamikanico.no 🕐 Daily 14.00–03.30.

Skansen It's not every bar that calls a closed-down public convenience home, but this one does. The atmosphere is unusual and the acoustics are not concert-hall quality. ➋ Rådhusgata 25. 🕐 Daily 12.00–03.00.

Summit 21 Enjoy the view along with your cocktail at this bar high on the 21st floor of the Radisson Hotel. ➋ Holbergs Gate 30 ➊ 23 29 30 00. Ⓦ www.radisson.com 🕐 Mon–Thur 16.00–01.00, Fri 16.00–02.00, Sat 16.00–02.30, Sun 17.00–01.00.

Tiger, Tiger for the young and dance-mad. ➋ Torggata 5. ➊ 22 33 62 77. Ⓦ www.oslo.tigertiger.no 🕐 Thur–Sat 23.00–03.30.

Grünerløkka & Grønland

Two pockets of eastern Oslo have been rapidly emerging as dynamic multi-cultural areas with an impressive array of nightlife and eateries. Grünerløkka has changed from a dingy and run-down part of town, mostly home to Oslo's immigrant population, into a trend-setting area. The cafés and restaurants have started to outgrow the area and have spilled into neighbouring Grønland. For locations, see the main city map, page 54.

SIGHTS & ATTRACTIONS

Oslo Spektrum

A venue for really large concerts, cultural and sporting events, this is where the Nobel Peace Prize Concert, the Norwegian Military Tattoo and the Oslo Horse Show are held. International artists such as Paul McCartney, Elton John and Sting also perform here when they tour Oslo.

🅐 Sonja Henies Plass 2. ☏ 22 05 29 00. 🆆 www.oslospektrum.no

CULTURE

Munch Museet (Edvard Munch Museum)

This is the largest collection of work by Edvard Munch. Just before his death, the artist bequeathed all the paintings in his possession to the City of Oslo. The collection is massive, containing some 1,100 paintings, 4,500 drawings and 17,000 prints. On display are several versions of *The Scream*, his best known work.

After the theft of one of only two painted versions of *The Scream* in 2004 the museum was closed for months while security was

⬤ *Grünerløkka has become one of the most vibrant parts of the city*

upgraded. The painting has never been recovered, nor has anyone been convicted of its theft, despite several arrests, and it is feared it has been destroyed.

Many of Munch's other paintings are frequently on loan to other museums, but with over 180 sq m (1937 sq ft) of exhibition space you won't feel even slightly deprived.

🅰 Tøyengata 53. 🕿 23 49 35 00. 🌐 www.munch.museum.no
🕒 Daily 10.00–18.00 Jun–Aug; Tues–Fri 10.00–16.00, Sat & Sun 11.00–17.00 Sept–May. Admission charge. 🚇 Any eastbound T-bane train from the city: Tøyen; Bus 20: Munch Museet.

Kunstindustrimuseet (Museum of Applied Art)

The Museum of Applied Art, established in 1876, is one of the oldest of its kind in Europe. It houses a fine collection of Norwegian and foreign crafts and fashions from the 17th century to the present. The prize of the collection is the Baldishol Tapestry, dating from 1200. This is the only surviving Norwegian tapestry that employed the

Gobelin technique from the Middle Ages. This national treasure was only found when the Baldishol Church in Hedmark county was demolished in 1879. The museum also contains silver, ceramics and furniture. ❸ St. Olavs Gate 1. ❶ 22 03 65 40.
Ⓦ www.nationalmuseum.no Ⓛ Tues, Wed & Fri 11.00–17.00, Thurs 11.00–20.00, Sat & Sun 12.00–16.00. Ⓝ T-bane: Nationaltheatret; Bus 33, 37 or 46: Nordahl Bruns Gate.

RETAIL THERAPY

The once working-class area by the Aker River has over the last decade become one of the most interesting areas of Oslo. The atmosphere generated by so many immigrant nationalities is both electric and eclectic. Take some time to discover the many small shops and delicatessens. The best hunting ground is the area near the main streets of Markveien and Thorvald Meyers Gate.

Bonaparte A little bit punk, a little bit goth, definitely avant garde. Clothing for both sexes. ❸ Markveien 59.

D'lirium Street fashion in all its hip-hop glory. ❸ Markveien 56

Fretex Indulge in something a little bit wild at this second-hand clothes store. ❸ Markveien 51.

TAKING A BREAK

Hotel Havana A quirky little delicatessen that will feed your soul as well as your stomach. Lots of exotic munchies. ❸ Thorvald Meyersgate 36.

Bagel & Juice Just what it claims – fresh bagels, fresh juices and some really good coffee. Open for breakfast, lunch and dinner. ⊕ Thorvald Meyers Gate 44.

Fru Hagen A trendy and arty sort of place serving international dishes until 21.30, when it turns into an upmarket bar. Be prepared for a long wait to get an outside table during the summer. ⊕ Thorvald Meyers Gate 40.

QBA is very cool, very hip and very wired. You can use one of their computers or access the internet via wireless connection. Try not to drop any of the nachos, wraps or salads onto your laptop. ⊕ Olaf Ryes Plass 4. ⊕ 08.00–01.00 daily.

Mucho Mas from the outside it looks a bit inauspicious but the food is top-notch Mexican. You'll find lots of tacos, burritos, nachos and plenty of beer to put out the fire from too many *chiles rellenos*. Note: credit cards are not accepted. ⊕ Thorvald Meyers Gate 36.

AFTER DARK

Restaurants
Punjab Tandoori K–KK Close to the Grønland T-bane station, this authentic restaurant will make you feel more as if you are in India than Norway. Samosas, dal and tasty curries that aren't too hot (unless you ask for them that way) make for a filling and not-too-expensive meal. ⊕ Gronlansleiret 24.

Sult K–KK is a really popular and very informal restaurant that is always, always packed to the rafters with hungry diners waiting to plough into platefuls of pasta and fish. Try and get there early or be prepared to wait. ⓐ Thorvald Meyers Gate 26

Bistro Bocante KK is an excellent choice for dining a la Francaise. In summer this Parisian styled little bistro has outdoor tables (which are always at a premium). The quiche and salads are always a good bet. ⓐ Thorvald Meyers Gate 40

Bars & clubs
Bar Boca Call it small or intimate, this is one of the coolest bars in Grünerløkka. Probably the best Mojito cocktail in town.
ⓐ Thorvald Meyersgate. ☎ 22 04 13 77. ⓦ www.barboca.no

Bia This is where Oslo comes to hear up and coming jazz artists. The fact that this is one of the prettiest settings in Oslo is a bonus.
ⓐ Brenneriveien 9c.

Café Kaos Another new addition to Grünerløkka's ever-expanding music scene. Great for summertime, with its large outside area.
ⓐ Thorvald Meyers Gate 56. ☎ 22 04 69 90 ⓦ www.cafékaos.no
🕑 Mon–Thur 16.00–03.30, Fri–Sat 14.00–03.30, Sun 014.00–22.00.

Gloria Flames A bar with a roof garden has got to be one the of the best places to try on a hot summer night. ⓐ Grønland 18.
☎ 22 17 16 00. ⓦ www.gloriaflames.no

Parkteatre Bar or Scene If you don't mind long queues you'll find this to be one of the hottest scenes in the city. ⓐ Olaf Ryes Plass 11.
☎ 22 35 63 00. ⓦ www.parkteatret.no 🕑 Daily 12.00–01.00.

◗ *Grünerløkka's the area for Oslo's coolest bars and clubs*

Bygdøy Peninsula

Bygdøy was an island until the end of the 19th century, when the sound between Frognerkilen and Bestumkilen was filled. Today this area is home to some of the finest museums and attractions in the city. The peninsula is easy to access from the city – just take the ferry that runs from the quay opposite the Rådhuset. There are also frequent bus connections from the city centre. You'll soon discover that the Bygdøy offers much more than cultural attractions. There are groves, meadows and parklands filled with a wealth of plant species. And, in summer, you'll find the beaches here to be one of Oslo's more popular places.

SIGHTS & ATTRACTIONS

Oscarshall

Every king needs a place to get away from it all and 19th-century King Oscar I was no exception. This residence was originally conceived to be a showcase of the architecture, art and handicrafts of the country. The castle is Norway's finest neo-Gothic building and was extensively renovated in 1929. Terraces with fountains lead down to the sea.

🅐 Oscarshallveien 805, Bygdøy. ☏ 22 56 15 39.
🅦 www.kongehuset.no 🕐 Wed–Sun. 12.00–16.00 Jun–mid-Aug, 12.00–16.00 mid-Aug–early Sept. 🚌 Bus 30: Kongsgården.

Ibsenmuseet (Ibsen Museum)

The home of Norway's most celebrated playwright has been lovingly and painstakingly restored to the decoration and furnishings of his period. This is the apartment occupied by Ibsen and his wife from

1895 until his death in 1906. Currently under reconstruction, the museum is scheduled to reopen on 23 May 2006.
ⓐ Museumsveien 10, Bygdøy. ☏ 22 12 37 00.
ⓦ www.norskfolkemuseum.no ⏰ Daily 09.00–20.00 15 May–14 Sept; 09.00–18.00 15 Sep–14 May. 🚌 Bus 30: Bygdøy; or a ferry from the City Hall pier (Aker Brygge) during the summer season.

Norske Folkemuseum (Norwegian Folk Museum)

More than 150 buildings gathered from all over Norway have been assembled to create Europe's largest open-air museum. Wander through centuries of everyday history as you visit farmhouses, market streets and churches. There's even a petrol station from the 1920s. The Gol Stave Church, adorned with paintings and carvings, has survived from the 12th century and is one of 30 such preserved churches in the country. Costumed guides play their roles and introduce you to bygone days. Annual events here include the Midsummer Eve Festival and the Christmas market in December.
ⓐ Museumsveien 10, Bygdøy. ☏ 22 12 37 00.
ⓦ www.norskfolke.museum.no ⏰ Mon–Fri 11.00–15.00, Sat & Sun 11.00–16.00, 2 Jan–14 May; daily 10.00–18.00, 15 May–14 Sept; Mon–Fri 11.00–15.00, Sat & Sun 11.00–16.00 15 Sept–30 Dec.
🚌 From downtown Oslo – Bus 30: Bygdøy, or a ferry from the City Hall pier (Aker Brygge) during the summer season.

Vikingshiphuset

The best preserved Viking ships ever found rest inside this museum. Built in the 9th century, these two burial ships are impressive to behold. The museum also houses Viking-era small boats, sledges, a

---

● *The quaint Gol Stave Church is one of the stars of the Norske Folkemuseum*

cart with exceptional ornamentation and household gear. These discoveries from Gokstad, Oseberg and Tune are the embodiment of the Viking spirit.

🅐 Huk Aveny 35, Bygdøy. 🕿 22 13 52 80. 🆆 www.khm.uio.no 🕓 Daily 11.00–16.00 Oct–Apr; 09.00–18.00 May–Sept. 🚍 Bus 30 or 30B: Vikingskipene; Ferry 91 from Rådhuskaia 3 (the City Hall Quay) to Dronningen (May–Sept).

Kon-tiki Museet

The exploits of Thor Heyerdahl held the world's interest in 1947 when he sailed his balsawood raft *Kon-tiki* across the vast reaches of the South Pacific in order to prove it would have been possible for South Americans to sail to Polynesia. The raft and artefacts of the voyage are on display. As if that feat wasn't enough, Heyerdahl sailed the *Ra II* across the Atlantic from Morocco to Barbados in 1970 and the *Tigris* across the Indian Ocean from Egypt to India in 1977. The museum also houses a collection of literature on Polynesia, with some 8,000 volumes.

🅐 Bygdøynesveien 36. 🕿 23 08 67 67. 🆆 www.kon-tiki.no 🕓 Daily. 10.30–16.00 Jan–Mar; 10.00–17.00 Apr–May; 09.00-17.30 Jun–Aug; 10.00–17.00 Sept–Oct; 10.30–16.00 Nov–Dec. 🚍 Bus 30B: Bygdøynes; Ferry 91 from Rådhuskaia 3 (the City Hall Quay) to Bygdøynes (May–Sept).

Frammuseet

Next door to the Kon-tiki Museum is the home of the polar ship *Fram*. Dating from 1892 and billed as 'the world's strongest ship', she has sailed to the North Pole and the far reaches of Antarctica. Used by explorers Nansen and Amundsen on their expeditions, the ship has been on display since 1936; you can board and walk round her to

● *This cart is part of the Viking heritage on display at Frammuseet*

see the preserved objects from those great voyages. The ship and the rest of the museum chart the unique contribution of these and other Norwegians to polar exploration and house equipment, photographs and paintings.

ⓐ Bygdøynesveien 36. ⓣ 23 28 29 50. Ⓦ www.fram.museum.no/en

⬭ *The Maritime and Fram Museums are enough to keep naval enthusiasts happy for days*

🕐 Daily. 10.00–15.45 Jan–Apr & Oct–Dec; 10.00–17.45 May–mid Jun; 09.00–18.45 mid Jun–Aug; 09.00–17.45 Sept. Ⓝ Bus 30B: Bygdøynes; Ferry 91 from Rådhuskaia 3 (City Hall Quay) to Bygdøynes, May–Sept.

Norsk Sjøfartsmuseum (Norwegian Maritime Museum)
Completing the trio of institutions in this corner of Bygdøy is this

museum displaying the history and traditions of Norwegian fishing, shipbuilding and marine archaeology. It is the shipbuilding, however, that is the key to Norway's culture. From the elegant ships of the early Viking explorers to the latter-day supertankers Norway has always been at the forefront of marine activity. The exhibit halls feature an abundance of model ships and the well stocked library contains a marvellous collection of drawings, photographs and literature.

ⓐ Bygdøynesveien 37. ❶ 24 11 41 50. Ⓦ www.norsk-sjofartsmuseum.no ⓒ Daily 10.00–18.00 mid-May –Aug; Mon–Wed 10.30–16.00, Thur 10.30–18.00, Fri–Sun 10.30–16.00 Sept–mid-May. Ⓝ Bus 30B: Bygdøynes.; Ferry 91 from Rådhuskaia 3 (the City Hall Quay) to Bygdøynes (May–Sept).

Sjømannskirken (Sailors' Church)

This is the Oslo Seaman's Mission, devoted to those who work on the ships and in the port of Oslo. It is used as a social centre as well as a church, and the grounds are home to the Seamen's Memorial, erected in 1966 to commemorate Norwegian sailors who have perished at sea.

ⓐ Nedre Slottsgate 4. ❶ 22 47 86 86. Ⓦ www.sjomannskirken.no

Hukodden

This hook-shaped promontory is home to Paradise Bay, perhaps the best beach and seaside park in Oslo. Because it is easily accessible from the city it positively teems with bathers on weekends. But if lying sardine-style on the beach isn't for you, there are plenty of walkways along the shore and through the adjoining woods. From the furthest point on the 'Huk' you'll get a terrific view of the of the Oslofjord, stretching from the Dyna lighthouse to Nesodlandet in

the south. If you prefer to sunbathe in the nude, head for the naturist beach to the north of Paradise Bay. The bay is only 15 minutes' walk from the museums of Bygdøy, and there's a restaurant on hand, too.

ⓐ Bygdøy ⓣ 22 43 74 62. ⓦ www.sult.no/inenglish1.cfm ⓒ Daily 12.00–22.00. ⓝ Bus 30: Bygdøy Huk; Ferry 91 from Rådhuskaia 3 (the City Hall Quay) to Bygdøynes (May–Sept).

RETAIL THERAPY

The best bet for shopping in the Bygdøy area are the gift shops in the various museums, which are filled to the brim with Norwegian handicrafts. In December the Christmas market that takes place at the Norsk Folkemuseum is not to be missed.

TAKING A BREAK

Najaden Restaurant K–KK A part of the Maritime Museum (Norsk Sjøfartsmuseum), this restaurant keeps the same hours as the attraction. The prices are reasonable and the selection is not outstanding but good for quick lunch. ⓐ Bygdøynesveien 37. ⓣ 22 43 81 80. ⓦ www.najaden.no

Dyna Fyr KKK A unique restaurant set in the Dyna lighthouse of Oslofjord. Reservations are an absolute must. You'll be picked up by boat in front of City Hall. Seafood is, of course, the mainstay of the menu. ⓐ Beddingen 6. ⓣ 22 43 60 12.

◀ *Heroic figureheads at the Maritime Museum*

THE CITY

Holmenkollen, Frogner & Majorstua

Much of what Oslo has to offer is north-west of the city centre.
Whether it is the sculptures in Frogner-Vigelands Park, the ski jump
at Holmenkollen, or some of the many museums in the suburbs, you
will want to budget some of your time to get outside the city
centre. Label-conscious party animals will feel right at home in the
west-end atmosphere of Majorstua and Frogner. Bogstadveien and
Hegdehaugsveien have an abundance of bars and pubs that party
long into the night. The efficient Oslo public transport system
makes it easy to visit all these places. For sights in Frogner, see the
map on page 91; other sights are on the main map, page 54.

SIGHTS & ATTRACTIONS

Holmenkollen
No trip to Oslo is complete without a trip to this world-famous ski
jump, if for no other reason than to enjoy its magnificent view of
the city. The ideal time to visit would be during one of the
competitions held there, but this means a winter trip, which is not
most visitors' preference. Fortunately, there are activities at
Holmenkollen all year round. You can try a ski simulator to get a feel
for the thrill of ski jumping, or you can visit the Ski Museum or study
some of the other ski-related exhibits on the site. If possible you
might want to plan a trip when one of the summer concerts is
being held there. There is a restaurant and an extensive gift and
souvenir shop on site.

The **Ski Museum**, dedicated to the sport of skiing, is located at
the foot of the Holmenkollen ski jump. It opened in 1923 and covers
over 4000 years of skiing history. Displays include the various types

○ *You can visit the top, but take a deep breath befoe you look down!*

of skis used, and the development of the different types of skiing event. There are also exhibits covering the Antarctic expeditions of Amundsen and Scott, and the Greenland expedition of Nansen. Norway's hosting of the Olympics in 1952 and 1994 is covered as well. The museum was recently expanded to include Norwegian paintings and other artwork connected with winter activities. ⓐ Kongeveien 5. ⓣ 22 92 32 00. ⓦ www.holmenkollen.com and www.skiforeningen.no ⓒ Daily 10.00–16.00 Oct–Apr; 10.00–17.00 May & Sept; 09.00–20.00 Jun; 09.00–20.00 Jul–Aug. ⓣ T-bane line 1: Holmenkollen. By car, it takes only 20 minutes to get to Holmenkollen area from the city centre: from Ring Road 3, exit at Smestad and follow the signposts to Holmenkollen. From the city centre, there are signposts from Majorstua to Holmenkollen.

Bogstad Herregard

An 18th-century farming estate that lies on the eastern bank of Bogstad Lake, Bogstad Herregard dates back to the Middle Ages and was owned by a series of famous and wealthy Norwegians before becoming an extension of the Norsk Folkemuseum in 1954. The current Manor House was built in the late 18th century by Peder Anker, who would later become Prime Minister. Most of the artwork and other artefacts date to that time. The beautiful English-style park and gardens surrounding the estate were also built by Peder Anker. The buildings have recently undergone extensive restoration. There are a café and a shop on site.

ⓐ Sorkedalen 826. ❶ 22 06 52 00. ⏱ Tues–Sun 12.00–16.00 mid May–mid-Oct. Ⓝ Bus 41.

Det Internasjonale Barnekunstmuseet (International Museum of Children's Art)

Founded in 1986 in association with SOS Children's Villages and featuring children's art from over 150 countries, the museum exhibits paintings, sculptures, ceramics, textiles and collages. Visiting children can participate in music, dance, painting and drawing, and there are also films, videos and workshops. There is a shop on site.

ⓐ Lille Frøens Vei 4. ❶ 22 46 85 73.
ⓦ www.english.barnekunst.no/default.htm ⏱ Tues–Thur & Sun 11.00–16.00 25 Jun–8 Aug; Tues–Thur 09.30–14.00, Sun 11.00–14.00, 15 Sept–24 Jun. Ⓝ T-bane line 1: Frøen; Bus 46.

Vigelandsparken

This large park (part of the much larger Frogner Park) is dedicated to sculptor Gustav Vigeland and contains 212 of his works. The

❶ Share Vigeland's astonishing visions at the park named after him

centrepiece is the 17 m (53 ft) high *Monolith*, with 121 human figures supporting each other. Other highlights are the bridge and the fountain. The park has tennis courts that are open in the summer and an adjacent public swimming pool. There is a visitor's centre and a café at the main entrance to the park.

ⓐ Kirkeveien. ❶ 23 49 37 00.

Ⓦ www.museumsnett.no/vigelandmuseet/eindex.htm

Ⓝ T-bane: All westbound lines: Majorstuen station; Bus 20 or Tram 12: Vigelandsparken.

Frognerseteren

This recreational area near Holmenkollen is the starting point for well marked hiking and skiing trails in the Nordmarka woods. Originally inhabited in 1790, it became public at the end of the 19th century when a traditional wooden lodge was built, which now houses the Tryvannstarnet restaurant. There is an observation tower, from which it is possible to see Sweden, as well as Oslo and the Oslofjord.

ⓐ Holmenkollveien 200. ❶ 22 92 40 40. ❺ Mon–Thur 12.00–16.00, Fri–Sun 10.00–16.00, Oct–Apr; daily 10.00–17.00 May & Sept; daily 10.00–19.00 July& Aug. Ⓝ T-bane line 1: Frognerseteren.

CULTURE

Vigelandsmuseet

The museum dedicated to Norway's great sculptor Gustav Vigeland lies just outside Vigelandsparken, and contains much of the artist's work. It was built in Norwegian Neo-Classical style, initially as a studio for the artist on the understanding that it would eventually become a museum containing his work.

The museum contains some 2700 sculptures, over 10,000 drawings and woodcuts and carvings. Vigeland's ashes are in the tower of the museum.

🅐 Nobelsgate 32. ☎ 23 49 37 00.

🆆 www.museumsnett.no/vigelandmuseet 🕑 Tues–Sun. 12.00–16.00 Sept–May, 11.00–17.00 Jun–Aug. 🚍 Bus 20 or 45, Tram 12: Frogner Plass. T-bane all westbound lines: Majorstuen.

Emanuel Vigeland Museum

This darkened, unusual building was once the studio of Emanuel Vigeland, the younger brother of Gustav, and is now his mausoleum as well as museum (his ashes are in an urn over the entrance door), and was opened to the public in 1958, 10 years after his death. Although renowned for his frescos and stained glass, Emanuel also painted and sculpted. On display is his *Vita*, a group of frescos that was considered very risqué and provocative when they were produced in the 1940s.

🅐 Grimelundsveien 8. ☎ 22 14 57 88.

🆆 www.emanuelvigeland.museum.no 🕑 Sun 12.00–16.00.

🚇 T-bane line 1: Slemdal; Bus 46: Grimelundsveien.

Oslo Bymuseum (City Museum)

Located in the Vigelandsparken, this 18th-century manor house is dedicated to the history of Oslo. All aspects of the city's history are depicted in models, pictures, room interiors and displays. There are three other buildings, which together with the museum form a traditional farm layout with an open square in the middle. The original manor encompassed the land which now makes up Frogner Park. There is a café and shop on site.

🅐 Frognerveien 67. ☎ 23 28 41 70. 🆆 www.oslobymuseum.no

🕐 Tues 10.00–19.00, Wed–Sun 10.00–18.00 15 Jan–23 Dec. Ⓝ T-bane all westbound lines Majorstuen; Bus 20 or Tram 12: Frogner Plass.

Private galleries

Galleri K Owned by Ben Fria, a noted authority on the works of Edvard Munch and many other Norwegian artists. Ⓐ Bjørn Farmannsgate 6. ☎ 22 55 35 88. 🔟 www.gallerik.com

Galleri JMS One of the best galleries in Oslo for contemporary art, by both Norwegian and international artists. Ⓐ Arbinsgate 3. ☎ 22 92 55 02. 🔟 www.gallerijms.no

RETAIL THERAPY

Between the Royal Palace and Vigeland Park is the retail shopping area of Majorstua. Most shops are on Hegdehaugsveien and Bogstadveien, and most shops feature designer and high-class clothing. In Frogner there are also designer clothing shops, and furniture shops. You will have no problem burning up your plastic here. The museum shops in this area offer some truly unique gifts and souvenirs so don't forget to take time to do some of your shopping while you're busy being a culture vulture.

Designagain A furniture store specialising in designs from the 50s, 60s and 70s. Ⓐ Hegdehaugsveien 22 ☎ 22 46 44 00. 🔟 www.designagain.no

Kamikaze Exclusive designer clothing for those on the cutting edge

⊙ *Majorstua is your best bet for designer shopping*

of style. ⓐ Hegdehaugsveien 24. ⓣ 22 60 20 25. ⓛ Mon–Wed 10.00–17.00, Thur 10.00–18.00, Fri 10.00–17.30, Sat 10.00–15.30.

Lille Vinkel sko Carries a variety of young and trendy shoes. ⓐ Kirkeveien 59. ⓣ 22 46 86 18. ⓦ www.lillevinkelsko.no ⓛ Mon–Wed, Fri: 09.00–18.00, Thur 09.00–19.00, Sat 10.00–17.00.

MA Noted for its exclusive designer clothing. ⓐ Hegdehaugsveien 27. ⓣ 22 60 72 90.

Skandinavisk Hoyfjellsutstyr A sports equipment store that features Norwegian brands such as Helly Hansen, Norrona, and Hjelle. You will also find sportswear lines from Olympic skiing champions Vegard Ulvang and Bjorn Daehlies. ⓐ Bogstadveien 1. ⓣ 22469075

Sprell Quality toy store for both the young and the young at heart. ⓐ Industrigaten 49. ⓣ 22 60 26 80.

Tonica Vintage As its name suggest, a store that specialises in vintage clothes. ⓐ Schoningsgate 14. ⓣ 22 60 22 06.

TAKING A BREAK

Frogner and Majorstua offer a wide variety of cafés and restaurants, some fairly exclusive, many catering to the young and trendy.

Café Elise K A cheerful and sunny little bistro with glass walls to really let the light shine in. Limited menu. ⓐ Elisenbergveien 22. ⓣ 22 44 25 11.

Frogner Konditori K After a long walk in the park you can relax and restore in this local café that features excellent baked goods. 🄰 Frognerveien 58. 🕔 24 11 90 00.

Pascal K Famous for its pastries and cakes that border on being works of art. Even Bill Clinton came to Pascal's to indulge in the goodies in the glass cases. 🄰 Drammensveien 10. 🕔 22 55 00 20.

Samson K A traditional corner bakery with a small café on site. A nice place to stop and put your feet up for a bit in between rounds of sightseeing. 🄰 Gyldenløves Gate 8. 🕔 22 54 23 60. 🕸 www.samson.no

Apent Bakeri K Don't say we didn't warn you! The freshly baked bread and just brewed coffee are simply irresistible. Don't be surprised to find a queue out of the door and down the street. 🄰 Inkognito Terr 1. 🕔 22 44 94 70.

Café M K–KK is a 5-minute walk from Vigelandsparken. There is a bar/café area, as well as a full restaurant, and an outdoor seating area for summer. Café M has a very complete food and drink menu. 🄰 Valkyriegt 9. 🕔 22 60 34 00. 🕸 www.cafem.no 🕒 Daily 11.00–01.00.

Herregardskroen K–KK In the Oslo Bymuseum in Frogner Park, this is a good place to get away from the hustle and bustle of the city. Surrounded by open space, large trees and Frogner Lake, it has good views of the park and of Holmenkollen. 🄰 Frognerveien 67. 🕔 22 43 77 30. 🕸 www.herregaardskroen.no 🕒 Daily 11.00–22.00 Easter–30 Sept.

AFTER DARK

The Majorstua and Frogner areas of Oslo are the trendiest and most expensive spots in the city. This is where you go to see and be seen. Dress your best and expect some long waits on the weekends unless you've made reservations in advance.

Etta Place Bar K You'll feel as if everyone knows your name with this bar's home-from-home ambiance.
ⓐ Hegdehaugsveien 30b. ⓣ 22 60 75 90.

Fuji K A tiny little hideaway with probably the best sushi in the city. Try and get a table upstairs where the atmosphere is a little more quiet. ⓐ Munkedamsveien 100. ⓣ 22 43 11 80.

Pizza Da Mimmo K It's not often that you need to make reservations for a low-budget pizzeria but the pizza here is so good that you have to. This casual and cosy place is one of the most popular eateries in Oslo. ⓐ Behrens Gate 2. ⓣ 22 44 40 20.

Clodion Art Café K–KK A colourful bar/café for those interested in art and the art scene in the city.
ⓐ Bygdøy Allé 63. ⓣ 22 44 97 26. ⓦ www.clodion.no

Havana Social Club K–KK Desperate smokers will find relief in the outdoor bar/pub setting of this pub. ⓐ Hegdehaugsveien 31.
ⓣ 22 46 02 00.

◉ *Head west to Frogner for Oslo's trendiest bars*

Hilarios Pub K–KK A good choice to have a beer in a warm and casual atmosphere. ⓐ Niels Juels Gate 38. ⓣ 22 43 63 90.

Horgans Bar & Restaurant K–KK An American-style sports bar for when you have to watch a game with your beer. ⓐ Hegdehaugsveien 24. ⓣ 22 60 87 87. ⓦ www.horgans.no

Frognerseteren KK This beautiful old log building exudes romance and has great views of the city, a cosy fireplace and really good food. ⓐ Holmenkollveien 200. ⓣ 22 92 40 40.

Hos Thea KK Warm and friendly restaurant with a large fireplace to give it that extra added glow. ⓐ Gabels Gate 11. ⓣ 22 44 68 74.

Palace Grill KK You can't make a reservation for this small, hip restaurant, so expect a bit of a wait, while watching Oslo's trendies on parade. ⓐ Solligate 2. ⓣ 23 13 11 40. ⓦ www.palacegrill.no

Bagatelle Restaurant KKK The only restaurant in Oslo with two stars in the Michelin Guide, so be prepared for steep prices. One of Oslo's in-spots, this eatery is as stylish as the food is gourmet. ⓐ Bygdøy Allé 3. ⓣ 22 12 14 40. ⓦ www.bagatelle.no

Holmenkollen Restaurant KKK The restaurant at the famous ski jump opened in 1892, but has recently undergone renovations. It has great views of Oslo and Oslofjord. The menu offers both Norwegian and international cuisine. ⓐ Holmenkollveien 119. ⓣ 22 13 92 00. ⓦ www.holmenkollen-restaurant.oslo.no

---

◗ *The Hurtigruten sweeps through magnificent fjord scenery*

OUT OF TOWN
trips

Oslo fjords & Bergen

If you travel to Oslo, you must take time to visit the fjords. And, with typical Norwegian efficiency, it is unbelievably easy to take in a few fjords, some spectacular countryside and a thrilling train ride all in a neat little package called, not surprisingly, 'Norway in a Nutshell®', which can be booked as a ready-made package (see
Ⓦ www.visitnorway.com).

You begin by departing Oslo on an 08.00 train for Bergen. The rail line sweeps out of the city and across the country's mountainous spine, with its deep forests, lakes and glaciers. The railway was completed in 1909 and is considered to be an engineering feat. It's 300 miles long and has some 300 bridges and 200 tunnels, all of which you will journey past in under 7 hours.

At Myrdal, a 12-mile spur line plunges down 900m (2800 ft) in just under an hour, to Flåm. This handy little town is really little more than a whistle stop for the train. You'll want to make a connection to Aurland, a charming country village a few miles north, whose speciality is *geitost* (goats cheese). If your train ride into Flåm hasn't satisfied your need for mountain scenery, take the train to Berkvam and hike or bike the gravel road back down to Flåm. Be sure to bring your own picnic.

From Flåm most 'nutshellers' catch one of the fjord cruises. Be prepared for 90 minutes of non-stop camera clicking as tourists scurry back and forth across the boat decks in quest of the perfect photo. The fjord walls are so close you'll feel as though you could reach out and touch them. Most boats travel up the narrow Aurlandsfjord and then down the Naeroyfjord to Gudvangen, where buses will shuttle you to the town of Voss. At Voss it's time to hop the train and proceed to Bergen, Norway's second city and historic

capital. You can finish the day there by browsing the touristy waterfront area, taking a harbour ferry, or zipping up the funicular to the top of the 320m (1000 ft) tall 'Mount' Fløyen for a view of the city. All too soon it's time to catch the overnight train back to Oslo. In just 24 hours you will have experienced the mountains, fjord and countryside of Norway – in a nutshell.

But don't think you can't spend a little longer time in any of those places. In fact, you really should spend more time in Bergen. Famous for its picture perfect wooden buildings at the Hanseatic wharf in old Bryggen, Bergen has a lot more to offer. Billing itself as the 'Gateway to the Fjords' Bergen is a historical international city that has small town charm. In the late Middle Ages, Bergen was the most populous and most important city in Norway. Later Bergen was the home of Edvard Grieg and Ole Bull.

BERGEN CARD

The Bergen Card gives free admission to most museums, free travel on local buses and the Floibanen funicular and free guided tours of Bergen, as well as reduced prices for other attractions, concerts and boat tours. It also includes free parking, so if you have a car, the card will almost pay for itself in parking fees. The card is available for 24 and 48 hour periods and can be purchased from the local tourist office, railway station, bus terminal and some hotels. Lower-price cards are available for children 3–15 years of age.

● *Bergen takes its name from the hills which rise directly behind it*

SIGHTS & ATTRACTIONS

Famous for its wooden buildings at the Hanseatic wharf in old Bryggen, Bergen has a lot more to offer. Billing itself as the 'Gateway to the Fjords', it is a historic international city with small-town charm. In the late Middle Ages, the city was the most populous and important in Norway. Among later claims to fame it was the home of composer Edvard Grieg.

Bryggen

Bryggen is a UNESCO World Heritage site. It is famous for its picture postcard-perfect wooden buildings with pointed gables facing the harbour. The area dates back to the 14th century, when Bergen joined the Hanseatic League and became a major northern trading centre. Bryggens Museum displays artefacts uncovered in archaeological digs from 1955 to 1972. It also shows the foundations of the city's oldest buildings on the original site. The chance to dig came after a disastrous fire in 1955 burned many of the buildings. Excavations under the burned ruins uncovered over a million items, including proof that the area had burned many times, from as early as 1170. **Bryggens Museum** ⓐ Dreggsalmenning 3. ⓣ 55 58 80 10. ⓦ www.uib.no/bmu ◷ Daily 10.00–17.00 May–Aug; Mon–Fri 11.00–15.00, Sat 12.00–15.00, Sun 12.00–16.00 Sept–Apr.

Hanseatic Museum

This is one of the best preserved wooden buildings in Bergen. Built in 1704, it is furnished to look like the home of a Hanseatic merchant in the 18th century. There are different areas for living quarters for the owner/manager and for the sailors and apprentices, as well as an area where fish were pressed and put in barrels.

📍 Finnegårdsgaten 1a. ☎ 55 54 46 90. 🌐 www.bergen.kommune.no
🕐 Daily 11.00–14.00 May; 09.00–17.00 Jun-Aug; 10.00–15.00 1–15
Sept; 11.00–14.00 16 – 30 Sept; Tues–Sat 11.00–14.00, Sun 12.00–17.00
Oct–Apr.

Håkonshallen (Haakon's Hall)

This medieval castle was built by King Haakon Haakonsson in the
mid-13th century, when Bergen was the political centre of Norway.
The castle was badly damaged in World War II but has been
extensively restored.
📍 Bergenhus Festning. ☎ 55 31 60 67. 🕐 Daily 10.00–16.00 mid-
May–Aug; 12.00–16.00 Sept–mid-May.

Rosenkrantztårnet (Rosenkrantz Tower)

The tower was built in the 1560's by Erik Rosenkrantz, governor of
Bergen at the time. It served as both a residence and as a fortified
tower for Bergen and incorporated earlier fortifications.
📍 Bergenhus Festning. ☎ 55 31 43 80. 🕐 Daily 10.00–16.00 mid-
May–Aug; Sun 12.00–15.00 Sept–mid-May.

THE HANSEATIC LEAGUE

This alliance of powerful German trading cities arose in the
Middle Ages and for long monopolised the profitable trade in
raw materials between Scandinavia, the Baltic states and
northern Europe. Its outposts reached as far as Riga and
Tallinn, and Bergen was its northernmost trading station.
Hanseatic merchants lived a rigid, monk-like existence,
forbidden to marry or dwell outside their trading colony.

Mariakirken (St Mary's Church)
This is the oldest building in Bergen; an outstanding Romanesque church, it was built of stone early in the 12th century. The pulpit was donated by Hanseatic merchants in 1676, and is considered an excellent example of baroque decorative art.

ⓐ Dreggen 15. ⓣ 55 31 59 60. ⓛ Mon–Fri 09.30–11.00 & 13.00–16.00 mid-May–Aug; Tues–Fri 11.30–13.30 Sept–mid-May

Views from above
There are great views to be enjoyed from the surrounding hills, which can be reached by funicular or cable car. Floibanen is a funicular that takes you up 320 m (1000 ft) to the top of Mt Fløyen, where you get a great view of Bergen. There are several hiking trials at the top, including one that lets you walk back down to the city. Ulriksbanen is a cable car takes you up 640 m (2100 ft) to the top of Mount. Ulriken, where there is a café, radio tower, hiking trails and a spectacular panoramic view of the city and surrounding fjords.

Floibanen ⓐ Vetrlidsalmenning 21. ⓣ 55 33 68 00. ⓛ Daily 07.30–24.00 May–Aug; Sun–Fri 07.30–23.00, Sat 08.00–23.00 Sept–Apr.

Ulriksbanen ⓐ Ulriken 1. ⓣ 55 20 20 20. ⓦ www.ulriken.no ⓛ Daily 09.00–19.00 May & Sept; 09.00–22.00 Jun–Aug; 10.00 – 17.00 in the winter – on sunny days.

CULTURE

Bergens Sjøfartsmuseum (Bergen Maritime Museum)
Like its counterpart in Oslo (see page 96), this museum tells the story of Norwegian shipping from early times to the modern day.

ⓞ *Take the Floibanen for breathtaking views of Bergen*

Established in 1921, it has a collection of models of Viking ships and other working boats.
ⓐ Haakon Sheteligs Plass 15. ☏ 55 54 96 00. ⓦ www.bsj.uib.no
🕐 Daily 11.00–15.00 Jun–Aug; Sun–Fri 11.00–14.00 Sept–May.

Norges Fiskerimuseum (Norwegian Museum of Fisheries)
Established in 1880, and is the oldest museum of its type in Norway. Displays show natural resources, management and products of the fishing industry that is still a major element in Norway's economy.
ⓐ Bontelabo 2. ☏ 55 32 12 49. ⓦ www.fiskerimuseum.no 🕐 Daily 10.00–18.00 Jun–Aug; Sun–Fri 11.00–16.00 Sept–May.

Buekorpsmuseet
This is dedicated to the Buekorps (Bow Corps), a boy's brigade known for its drills with crossbows. The museum has photographs and other items showing 150 years of activities.
ⓐ Murhvelvingen. ☏ 55 23 15 20. ⓦ www.buekorps.museum.no
🕐 Sat 11.00–14.00, Sun 12.00–15.00 mid-Aug–mid-Jul.

Bergen Kunstmuseum
The Bergen Art Museum includes several collections, as well as paintings by Munch and Picasso. The adjoining Bergen Kunsthall features changing art exhibits.
ⓐ Rasmus Meyers Allé 3, 7 & 9. ☏ 55 56 80 00.
ⓦ www.bergenartmuseum.no 🕐 Daily 11.00–17.00 mid-May–mid-Sept; Tues–Sun 11.00–17.00, mid-Sept–mid-May.

Vestlandske Kunstindustrimuseum
The West Norway Museum of Decorative Art has several permanent

collections as well as changing exhibits. The museum features one of the world's oldest and most beautiful violins, which dates back to 1562. It was played by Norwegian virtuoso Ole Bull, another illustrious musical son of Bergen.

ⓐ Nordahl Bruns Gate 9. ❶ 55 33 66 33. Ⓦ www.vk.museum.no ❶ Daily 11.00–17.00 mid-may–Mid-Sept; Tues–Sun 12.00–16.00 mid-Sept–mid-May.

Bergen Museum

De Naturhistoriske Samlinger (Natural History Collections) is a botanical garden with a partially restored old zoological collection. There are also geological and botanical exhibits. De Kulturhisoriske Samlinger (Bergen Cultural History Collections) range from antiquity through the middle ages and up to the present day. Included are archaeological finds, textiles, history records and an ethnographic collection

Bergen Museum Ⓦ www.bergenmuseum.uib.no ❶ Tues–Fri 10.00–14.00, Sat & Sun 11.00–15.00, Sept–May; Tues–Fri 10.00–16.00, Sat & Sun 11.00–16.00 Jun–Aug.
De Naturhistoriske Samlinger ⓐ Museplass 3. ❶ 55 58 29 49.
De Kulturhistoriske Samlinger ⓐ Haakon Sheteligsplass 10.
❶ 55 58 31 40.

Grieghallen

Bergen's concert hall is named after its most famous citizen, composer Edvard Grieg. It is Norway's largest auditorium. The Bergen Philharmonic Orchestra, founded in 1765, performs here every Thursday evening from September to May.

ⓐ Edvard Griegs Plass 1. ❶ 55 21 61 00. Ⓦ www.grieghallen.no

Den Nationale Scene (Norwegian National Theatre)

Founded in 1850 by Ole Bull, Bergen's famed violinist, the theatre is currently housed in an art nouveau building that is a landmark in the centre of Bergen. Henrik Ibsen was a director here for six years from 1851. ⓐ Engen 1. ⓣ 55 54 97 00. ⓦ www.den-nationale-scene.no

Kulturhuset

This former sardine factory has been converted to Bergen's main cultural centre, with a full range of contemporary arts such as music, film, dance and theatre.
ⓐ Georgernes Verft 12. ⓣ 55 31 55 70. ⓦ www.kulturhuset-usf.no

RETAIL THERAPY

Bergen has always been a trading centre, and today is no different.

● *Bryggen carries on Bergen's centuries-old commercial traditions*

There is no shortage of places to shop, from small and specialised shops to large department stores and malls.

Galleriet is a shopping mall with over 70 outlets covering most needs. Clothes, books, cafés, a pharmacy, souvenirs and art galleries are all here. ❸ Torgallmenningen 8. ❶ 55 30 05 00.

Bergen Storsenter is Bergen's largest shopping centre with over 70 stores selling most commodities, as well as services such as dentists and a pharmacy. There are indoor walkways to bus, train and car park. ❸ Stromgaten 8. ❶ 55 21 24 60.

Bryggen Husflid A/S has a very large selection of hand-knit sweaters from Norsk Handstrikk, Dole of Norway, Nordtrikk and Skjaeveland. They also sell souvenirs, cuddly trolls and more. ❸ Bugarden. ❶ 55 32 88 03.

Nilssen pa Bryggen carries a large selection of knitwear, wool, textiles and embroidery. They are conveniently located at the wharf next to the Hanseatic Museum. ⓐ Bryggen 3. ⓣ 55 31 67 90.

Christmas Shop is, as its name suggests, an all-year Christmas shop with a large selection of typical *nisse* (Norwegian Santa Clauses). ⓐ Bryggen. ⓣ 55 21 51 00.

Glass Thomsen specialises in glass, crystal, dinner sets and gift articles. They have skilled staff and good service. ⓐ Strandgaten 64. ⓣ 55 53 94 50.

Kloverhuset is Norway's oldest shopping centre and Bergen's leading fashion house. It consists of many small and interesting shops with distinctive character. ⓐ Strandgaten 13/15. ⓣ 55 31 37 90.

Ruben's Varme Gleder is a store that carries toys, games, educational materials, costumes and souvenirs. The shop is near the fish market and the funicular. ⓐ Vetrlidsalmenning 5. ⓣ 55 31 41 11.

Troll is a small shop that specialises in trolls of varying sizes, shapes and materials. ⓐ Bryggen. ⓣ 55 21 51 00.

Viking is a small shop that specialises in Viking-inspired souvenirs, including replica of swords found in Viking graves (you might have trouble carrying them back on your plane). ⓐ Bryggen. ⓣ 55 21 51 00.

Bergen Steinsenter specialises in jewellery and watches, as well as objects made of stone and minerals. This is a good place to find an original ornament or gift. ⓐ Bredsgarden. ⓣ 55 32 82 60.

TAKING A BREAK

Baker Brun K don't leave Bergen without trying a *skillingsboller* (cinnamon bun) from this little bakery in the Brygge area. You can always walk a few extra miles to work off these delicious calories. 🅐 Damsgårdsvei 109a. ☎ 55 34 96 00.

Dr Livingstone Travellers Café K–KK As the name hints, this place features a spicy menu of foods from around the globe. Just perfect for when you can't decide on a specific cuisine for lunch. Open for lunches, coffee and into the evening. 🅐 Kong Oscarsgate 12. ☎ 55 56 03 12.

Fincken-Café K–KK Bergen's only café for the gay and lesbian crowd. Open every day, it serves as a restaurant during the early hours and as a pub in the evening hours. Very crowded. 🅐 Nygårdsgaten 2a ☎ 55 32 13 16.

Kafe Kippers USF K–KK This café at the Kulturhuset is, naturally, a gathering spot for local artists and artisans. The menu is international in flavour and the prices are affordable. The outdoor restaurant is one of Bergen's largest, with a great view of the city fjord. 🅐 Georgenes Verft 3. ☎ 55 31 00 60.

Sostrene Hagelin K–KK Opened in 1929 and still serving up dishes the same way – with fresh haddock only. You can eat in or take away for a picnic. 🅐 Olav Kyrresgate 33. ☎ 55 32 01 12.

Terminus Kafe K–KK one of the best places in Bergen for sandwiches and cakes. There is also a small menu of hot foods and a daily dinner special. 🅐 Zander Kaaesgate 6. ☎ 55 21 25 00.

AFTER DARK

Restaurants

Bryggens Tracteursted KK A modern twist on traditional Norwegian food. Set in the historic Hanseatic wharf area.
ⓐ Bryggestredet 2 ❶ 55 33 69 99

Zachariasbryggen Restauranter K–KK Right in the heart of the historic wharf area, this outdoor restaurant is a great place to soak up the local atmosphere. Local food and a good selection of local beers. ⓐ Torget 2. ❶ 55 55 96 40.

Fløyen Restaurant KK–KKK Originally opened in 1925, this distinctive bit of Bergen offers not only an innovative, and somewhat expensive, menu but some amazing views of the city. Be sure to ask for a window seat when you make the (necessary) reservation.
ⓐ Fløyfjellet 2. ❶ 55 32 18 75.

Bars & clubs

American Bar A classic bar for thirty-somethings in the Radisson Hotel. Join the convention crowd for a cold one. ⓐ Nedre Ole Bulls Plass 4. ❶ 55 57 30 33.

Blue Velvet Bar Youthful crowd with loud music. ⓐ Vågsallm 16.
❶ 55 55 49 68.

Café Clue Trendy Upmarket bar, a good place to see and be seen.
ⓐ Chr Michelsensgate 4. ❶ 55 32 59 00.

◗ *Linger over a coffee and a pastry at Baker Brun*

Dyvekes Vinkjeller Named after the mistress who became the Queen of Norway and Denmark. Intimate wine cellar with a good selection of reasonably priced wines. Very popular with locals. ⊕ Hollendergate 7. ☎ 55 32 30 60.

Engelen A little something for everyone. Oldies on Wednesday nights, disco on Thursdays, and the weekends are given over to R&B, soul, and hits from the 80s. ⊕ Bryggen ☎ 55 54 30 00.

Kamelon A fully-licensed bar with a vibrant musical scene. Expect young crowds. ⊕ Vågsalmenning 16. ☎ 40 00 59 15.

Rick's Café og Salonger Drinks, dancing and food. A large and popular club that hosts both DJ's and live concerts. ⊕ Øvre Ole Bulls Plass 9. ☎ 55 55 31 31.

Wessel Pub For decades this has been one of the most popular pubs in Bergen. Informal and always packed to the rafters. ⊕ Ole Bulls Plass 6. ☎ 55 90 07 39.

ACCOMMODATION

Alver Hotel K–KK Modern hotel with fully equipped rooms, just a little outside the city. ⊕ 5911 Alversund.
☎ 56 34 38 00. ⓦ www.alverhotel.no

Augustin Hotel KK–KKK Bergen's oldest family-run, full-service hotel integrates modern amenities with good old-fashioned service. All rooms have TV, telephone, hairdryers, and trouser press; they include non-smoking rooms and some adapted for travellers with

disabilities. 🅐 C. Sundtsgate 22–24. 🛈 55 30 40 00.
🅦 www.augustin.no

Best Western Hotel Victoria KK–KKK In the heart of the city, very
close to the railway station. Non-smoking rooms are available.
Standard amenities such as TV and hairdryer in every room. Internet
connection is available. 🅐 Kong Oscarsgate 29. 🛈 55 21 23 00.
🅦 www.victoriahotel.no

Comfort Hotel Holberg KK–KKK Set in a traditional area of the city
with timbered buildings, only about 5 minutes from the city centre
and wharf area. Enjoy a free breakfast in the morning, and in the
afternoon you can make your own waffles. There is also a health
club with sauna, steam bath and solarium. 🅐 Strandgaten 190.
🛈 55 30 42 00. 🅦 www.choice.no

Golden Tulip Rainbow Hotel Rosenkrantz KKK A traditional hotel
with excellent service. A restaurant, café and bar are located on the
premises. 🅐 Rosenkrantz Gaten 7. 🛈 55 30 14 00.
🅦 www.rainbow-hotels.no

Scandic Bergen City KKK A modern conference-style hotel with large
and comfortable rooms. 🅐 Håkonsgaten 2. 🛈 55 30 90 80.
🅦 www.scandic-hotels.no/bergencity.

Hurtigruten

Everyone's image of Norway focuses on the fjords that slice deeply into its western shore, creating one of the world's most spectacular coastlines. The midnight sun can be seen from late May to mid-July. From September to April the Northern Lights perform brilliant shows in the dark sky, although daylight hours are very short: from mid-November to mid-January the sun never rises.

Beautiful fjord scenery is just one reason for taking the legendary coastal voyage on Norway's Hurtigruten line. The name translates as 'fast route' and these coastal steamers were once the only connection between Norway's northern coastal towns. Today's modern ships still provide local transport, as well as being popular cruises. From almost any place on the ships passengers can watch the changing panorama of mountains, islands, fjords and little fishing harbours. Even without all the cruise-ship niceties, it would be an outstanding trip for the scenery and to be a part of local life in these remote North Sea communities. For an outline of the route, see the map on page 115.

While day-passengers can use this as transport to remote coastal towns and islands, most travellers take the entire route, either from Bergen to Kirkenes or vice versa. Some do both, because the ship makes daytime stops on the southbound trip where it stopped at night on the way north. An added attraction is a visit to the stunning Geirangerfjord on summer northbound sailings. Optional excursions are reasonably priced, often leaving the ship at one stop and travelling overland to re-board at a later port. Especially worthwhile are those to the North Cape, Vesteralen and Lofoten islands.

▶ *Arctic Tromsø is a picturesque stop on the route of the Hurtigruten*

Port stops vary from 15 minutes to several hours. In Vardø passengers follow a costumed drummer to the octagonal Vardøhus Fort, built in the 1700s, for sea views and tours of its historic buildings. In Stokmarknes, the Hurtigruten Museum recalls the service's founding here in 1893. Ålesund, where the ship stops at night on its southern voyage, is worth staying up for. Its art nouveau centre is floodlit and only a short walk from the dock. One of the beauties of the Norwegian Coastal Voyage is its flexibility. The ships sail all year, departing every day. Options range from cruise-only 6-day trips from Kirkenes to Bergen to 17-day packages that combine a 12-day return-trip with days to explore Bergen and Oslo.

Schedules and bookings ⓦ www.hurtigruten.com (UK and international); www.norwegiancoastalvoyage.us (North America).

SIGHTS & ATTRACTIONS

North Cape

Europe's northernmost point is more than simply a geographical landmark. The continent ends here with a bang, in a sheer drop into jagged rocks and crashing waves. Fog frequently envelops the cape, and in the early morning of a summer day, sun plays with fog to create a constantly changing land- and seascape. The glass-enclosed Nordkapphallen (North Cape Hall) has exhibits describing local wildlife and the dramatic story of the World War II Battle of North Cape. If you've a taste for chilled champagne you can have it here at the world's northernmost champagne bar.

Nordkapphallen ⊜ Honningsvåg. ⓣ 78 47 68 60.
ⓦ www.visitnorthcape.no ⓛ Daily Apr–mid-Oct; at other times for arrival of daily bus tour (ⓣ 78 47 70 30).

Hammerfest

The small city was levelled in World War II, when it was the headquarters for the German fleet in the North Atlantic. The crypt of Hammerfest Church was the only structure to survive, and one entire end wall of the striking new church is now a stained glass window. A museum of the reconstruction, Gjenreisningsmuseet, explores the forced evacuation of Hammerfest and the Germans' 'scorched earth' policy in the region during World War II, as well as the town's struggle to rebuild their homes and community after the war, some of the reconstruction by German volunteers. The Royal and Ancient Polar Bear Society is a favourite stop for its small displays recording the town's relationship with this arctic creature as well as its history since the 1600s as a centre for traders from Russia, the Arctic and as far away as southern Europe. You can join, earning the right to wear the club emblem.

Gjenreisningsmuseet ⓐ Kirkegata 21, Hammerfest. ⓘ 78 42 26 30. ⓦ www.museumsnett.no/gjenreisningsmuseet ⓛ Mon–Fri 09.00–14.00, Sat–Sun 10.00–14.00 mid-Jun–mid-Aug, daily 11.00–14.00 in winter. Admission free in winter.

Royal and Ancient Polar Bear Society ⓐ Rådhusplassen 1, Hammerfest. ⓘ 78 41 31 00.

Tromsø

Walk straight up the hill from the harbour to reach the busy main street, Storgata, kept lively by the city's large student population. Almost untouched by World War II, Tromsø retains the largest collection of 19th-century wooden buildings north of Trondheim. A particularly good group known as Skansen is near the harbour.

There are plenty of other sightseeing highlights. The Polar Museum in the heart of the old town is a preserved 1830s customs

building housing low-tech exhibits on polar exploration. Polaria, a multi-faceted discovery centre: learning experiences centre around polar regions, with films, sea aquarium, live seals and polar research exhibits. The Arctic Botanical Garden is a good introduction to the flora of this harsh region. Those interested in local Sami, prehistoric and Viking culture, as well as the nature and history of northern Norway, should spend an hour or two at the outstanding University Museum. It includes some of the many ancient rock carvings found nearby, and the Viking area has a full-sized replica Viking longhouse. Finally, to appreciate the city's splendid setting between the mountains and sea, ride the Fjellheisen cable car up to Storsteinen, 380 m (1200 ft) above.

Tourist Office ⓐ Stortorget 61. ⓣ 77 61 00 00.
ⓦ www.destinasjontromso.no ⓛ Daily mid-May–mid-Sept; Mon–Sat mid-Sept–mid-May.

Polaria ⓐ Hjalmar Johansensgate 12. ⓣ 77 75 01 00.
ⓦ www.polaria.no ⓛ Daily. 10.00—19.00 mid-May–mid-Aug; 12.00—17.00 mid-Aug–mid-May.

Polar Museum ⓐ Søndre Tollbugate 11. ⓣ 77 68 43 73.
ⓦ www.polarmuseum.no ⓛ Daily. 11.00–17.00 Mar–mid-Jun; 10.00–19.00mid-Jun–mid-Aug; 11.00–17.00 mid-Aug–Sept; 11.00–15.00Oct–Feb.

Arctic Botanical Garden ⓦ www.uit.no/botanisk. ⓝ Bus 20 to the university in Breivika.

University Museum Tromsø ⓐ Lars Thørings Veg 10. ⓣ 77 64 50 00.
ⓦ www.tmu.uit.no ⓛ Daily. 09.00–21.00 mid-Jun–mid-Aug; 09.00–18.00 mid-May–mid-Jun & mid-Aug–mid-Sept. Mon–Fri 09.00–15.30, Sat & Sun 11.00–17.00 mid-Sept–mid-May.

Fjellheisen cable car ⓐ Sollivn 12. ⓣ 77 63 87 37.
ⓦ www.fjellheisen.no. ⓛ Daily Apr–Sept, Sat & Sun Mar. ⓝ Bus 26.

Harstad, Vesteralen

Hurtigruten passengers on the Coastal Express can opt for a shore excursion to explore the scenic Vesteralen region by land, stopping at the medieval Trondenes Church in Harstad. Its unusual rood screen holds a painted pulpit, and the three altars have polychrome carved wooden statues. Visitors staying over in the area can also visit the interesting Trondenes Historical Centre, telling the story of the area from the Viking period and Middle Ages to World War II, with signage in English. Recent history is even more vividly told on a hill above town, where in a completely restored fortification is the enormous Adolf Gun, the world's largest land-based gun, built by the Germans in World War II. The small islands, connected by ferries, form a major agricultural area famed for highly-flavoured strawberries, which ripen in August.

Vesteralen Reiseliv (Tourist Office) ➌ Kjopmannsgata 2, Sortland. ➊ 76 11 14 80. Ⓦ www.visitvesteralen.com. ◖ All year.

Trondenes Historical Centre ➌ Harstad. 77 01 89 89. ◖ Tours June–mid-Aug 11.00, 13.00, 15.00, 17.00.

Trondheim

The main attractiions of Trondheim are the beautiful Nidaros Cathedral and walking through the streets lined with old houses. The earliest parts of the cathedral date from 11th century, and the statues in the spectacular facade surrounding the rose window date from the Middle Ages to the 1980s. Highlights include the magnificent organ in the north transept and the St Olaf painted altar front (1300). The world's first bicycle lift, near Gamle Bybro, the picturesque 1618 bridge, saves cyclists the long climb to Kristiansten Fort. More than 60 historic buildings form Trøndelag Folk Museum, among them a stave church from 1170.

Trondheim Activum (Tourist Office)  Torget, Trondheim. 73 80 76
60. www.visit-trondheim.com. Mon–Fri 09.00–16.00, Sat
10.00–14.00 in winter, longer in summer.

Trøndelag Folk Museum Sverresborg, Trondheim. 73 89 01 00.
Daily 11.00–18.00 Jun–Aug; Mon–Fri 11.00–15.00, Sat–Sun
12.00–16.00 Sept–May. Bus 8.

RETAIL THERAPY

Gjenreisningsmuseet (Reconstruction Museum) Shop Crafts,
including hand-made candles, are sold in the museum shop, along
with books and souvenirs. Kirkegata 21, Hammerfest. 78 42 26
30.

Royal and Ancient Polar Bear Society The little gift shop is a perfect
place to buy furry white toy bears for tots, as well as books and
souvenirs on Arctic and polar bear themes. Rådhusplassen 1,
Hammerfest. 78 41 31 00.

Galleri Nordnorge The local artists' association operates this
permanent gallery of the Festival of North Norway. Along with
paintings and drawings are fine crafts. Normannsgata 1A,
Harstad. 77 02 62 51. www.gallerin.no Tues–Sun 12.00—15.00.

Blast Visit this glassblowing workshop to see beautiful and useful
glassware being made. Hansensgate 4, Tromsø.
77 68 34 60. www.blaast.no Tues–Fri 10.00–17.00, Sat
10.00–15.00 (may vary with season).

Julehuset Gasa It's Christmas all year round at this shop filled with

Norwegian holiday decorations and traditions. ❸ Øvre Bakklandet 58, Trondheim. ❶ 73 50 50 30. ⏰ Mon–Fri 10.00–17.00, Sat 10.00–15.00 Mar–Dec.

TAKING A BREAK

Bakeriet Selskapsmat A friendly bakery/café. ❸ Prinsensgate 19, Trondheim. ❶ 72 84 59 90.

G Bar/café with a friendly atmosphere and good bagels. ❸ Storgata 49, Tromsø. ❶ 77 68 25 80.

Gjenreisningsmuseet (Reconstruction Museum) Caféteria Fresh-made waffles, coffee, hot cocoa and cakes are served in the museum's tidy little café. ❸ Kirkegata 21, Hammerfest. ❶ 78 42 26 30. ❾ www.museumsnett.no/gjenreisningsmuseet ⏰ Mon–Fri 09.00–14.00, Sat & Sun 10.00–14.00 mid-Jun–mid-Aug; Daily 11.00–14.00 in winter.

Kaffistova Home-style Norwegian cooking in a casual restaurant-café. ❸ Rik Kaarbosgate 6, Harstad. ❶ 77 06 12 57.⏰ Mon–Fri 08.00–18.00, Sat 11.00–15.00, Sun 11.30–16.30.

AFTER DARK

Look to swinging Tromsø for nightlife, although its nickname 'the Paris of the North' may be an exaggeration. Storgata is where the action is – and you can forget city dress codes. The small coastal town's nightlife is mostly low-key. You might see some unusual menu choices, such as seaweed, seagull eggs and seal lasagne!

Bryggerie K 'The northernmost microbrewery in the world', with live music and karaoke at weekends. ⓐ Nordkappgata 1, Honningsvåg (North Cape). ⓣ 78 47 26 00. ⓛ Daily 10.00–02.00 Jun–Aug.

Orens Kro KK This 1863 tavern keeps its cosy old-time atmosphere, while being a popular meeting place for young professionals who work in the riverside neighbourhood. Drinks, light dishes and an à la carte dinner menu. ⓐ Dokkgata 8, Trondheim. ⓣ 73 60 06 35.

Ovenpa KK Weekends are hottest, Thursday is club night, with lower prices on beer and wine. The DJ can spin anything: disco, techno, rock. ⓐ Stortorget 4, Tromsø. ⓣ 77 68 44 42.

Markens Grode KK–KKK The upscale menu in this elegantly furnished dining room revolves around the abundant local seafood and wild game of the region. There's also a wine bar and jazz and classical music. ⓐ Storgata 30, Tromsø. ⓣ 77 68 25 50.

Peppermollen KK–KKK Fish tops the menu at this very traditional and historic restaurant, a favourite of locals. Students love the restaurant's 'brown café' for its light meals (from the same excellent kitchen) and good espresso. ⓐ Storgata 42, Tromsø. ⓣ 77 68 62 60.

Restaurant Kompasset KK–KKK Traditional Norwegian dishes using, where possible, locally produced ingredients from Finnmark. ⓐ North Cape Hall, Honningsvåg. ⓣ 78 47 68 60. ⓛ Daily 17.00–24.00 mid-Jun–mid-Aug.

ⓓ *A reminder of Viking ships on Bygdøy's waterfront*

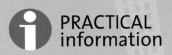

Directory

GETTING THERE

By air

SAS Braathens have code-sharing flights to Gardermoen serving no less than 11 UK cities – Aberdeen, Belfast, Birmingham, Edinburgh, Glasgow, Leeds, London (City, Gatwick and Heathrow), Manchester and Newcastle – as well as Dublin in the Republic of Ireland. Similar arrangements between SAS Braathens and major European and US airlines offer flights from many US cities. British Airways fly direct to Gardermoen from London Heathrow and Manchester, and from London Stansted there are also direct flights on Norwegian Airlines.

Ryanair connects the UK to Oslo Sandefjord Torp from London Stansted, Glasgow Prestwick, Liverpool and Newcastle.

SAS Braathens www.sasbraathens.no

British Airways www.ba.com

Norwegian Airlines www.norwegian.no

Ryanair www.ryanair.com

By rail

All international trains arrive at and depart from Oslo S. A direct journey from the UK by rail will involve a cross-Channel ferry or the Eurostar to Brussels as the first leg of your journey. From London (Waterloo International) to Oslo S will take 24–30 hours, via Brussels, Cologne, Hamburg, Copenhagen and Malmö or, with fewer changes of train, via Brussels, Cologne, Copenhagen and Göteborg (Gothenburg). The monthly *Thomas Cook European Rail Timetable* has up-to-date schedules for international train services to Oslo and many Norwegian domestic routes.

Eurostar Reservations (UK) ☎ 08705 186186 Ⓦ www.eurostar.com

Thomas Cook European Rail Timetable ⓣ (UK) 01733 416477; (USA) 1 800 322 3834. ⓦ www.thomascookpublishing.com

By ferry

Fjordline sail from Newcastle to Bergen on two routes, departing on either Saturdays or on Fridays and Sundays, depending on the route. DFDS ferries also depart from Newcastle on Fridays but arrive at Kristinsand, south of Oslo. In all cases the trip is an overnight one.
Fjordline www.fjordline.co.uk
DFDS Seaways www.dfds.co.uk

Driving

Oslo can be reached by car by using Highway E18 from the east or west, or Highway E6 from the north or south. With the opening of the Oresund bridge between Sweden and Denmark, it is now possible to reach Norway from the Channel ports without using a ferry. The roads in Norway are generally in good condition and well maintained, especially those in and around Oslo. If travelling in winter, check the road conditions before you leave. The wearing of seatbelts is mandatory, as is the use of headlights at all times of day. Children 12 years and younger must ride in the rear seat. Driving under the influence of alcohol is not tolerated, with the legal limit being 0.02 per cent, and jail sentences and large fines common.

The minimum age for driving is 18 years, and drivers must have a full national driving licence or an International Driving Permit. Vehicles entering Norway must have proof of registration and proof of insurance. Speed limits on highways are 80–100 kph (50–60 mph), in cities 50 kph (30 mph), with some residential areas at 30 kph (18 mph). Speed limits are rigorously enforced, speed traps are abundant and the fines are high, so watch your speed.

ENTRY FORMALITIES
Documentation

Citizens from the EU and most English-speaking countries can visit Norway for up to three months without obtaining a visa. If arriving by car, all drivers must have a national driving licence, or an International Driving Permit. Licences must be carried at all times, as well as automobile registration documents, and a valid certificate of insurance.

MONEY

Norway is not a member of the EU and has kept its traditional currency, the Norwegian Krone (Kr, usually shown in foreign exchange listings as NKR). The Krone is made up of 100 Ore. Some shops, especially in the tourist areas, may take euros and US dollars, but the practice is not common. Banks, ATMs and currency exchange kiosks are common throughout Oslo. All major credit cards are honoured at most shops and restaurants, as are euro, US dollar and UK sterling traveller's cheques.

HEALTH, SAFETY & CRIME

By international standards, Norway is a very healthy and safe country. Health standards are high; the water is safe to drink and the food safe to eat, although you might want to stay clear of *lutefisk* (see page 26). The biggest health concerns are flu and colds in winter, and sunburn and insect bites in summer. If you plan on hiking in the great outdoors, it would be wise to be vaccinated against tick-borne encephalitis.

Norway is a member of the European Economic Agreement, and thus has free reciprocal health agreements with all EU countries. Those that qualify need to carry their EHIC card. The Norwegian

Health Plan does not cover other nationals, but some countries' plans may cover all or part of medical costs in Norway, so visitors should check on this before departing for Norway. The costs of health care in Norway are quite reasonable compared to other Western countries, but non-EU visitors should carry adequate travel health insurance, and it is recommended even for visitors from within the EU.

Local pharmacies and medical centres can give advice and sell medications for most minor ailments. Most medical professionals in Norway speak good English.

The crime rate in Oslo is low, and it is considered one of the safest capital cities in the world. However, normal precautions should be taken to avoid pickpockets, purse snatchers and other petty criminals. Oslo has a growing drug problem, so beware of addicts, drunks and beggars. Police officers are easily identified by their black boots and trousers (trousers have a checkered trim), light blue shirts, and black caps with a police crest. Police cars and police stations are clearly marked POLICI. The police are normally unarmed, and are very friendly, helpful and courteous, so do not hesitate to ask them for information or directions. Cars should be locked and parked in open or well lit areas, with any valuables such as jewellery, cameras, mobile phones and computers locked in the trunk or otherwise out of sight.

OPENING HOURS

Banks are open Monday–Friday, normally 08.15–15.00 except Thursday, when they stay open until 17.00. Most shops operate Monday–Saturday, normally 10.00–17.00. On Thursday they stay open until 19.00, but on Saturdays close early at 14.00. Supermarket hours are 09.00–21.00 except Saturday, when they close at 18.00.

Restaurants generally open for breakfast (where served) 08.00–11.00, for lunch 12.00–15.00 and for dinner 18.00–23.00. Most museums open at 11.00 and close at 17.00, unless otherwise stated in this book. Some open earlier in the day, especially in summer.

TOILETS

Norway uses western-style toilets. Public toilets can be found at shopping malls, railway stations and bus stations, but in most cases you will have to pay up to 10Kr. to use them. A few restaurants still charge to use the facilities, although most do not. Toilets at libraries and museums are normally free.

CHILDREN

Travelling with children in Norway is quite easy. Many restaurants offer children's menus, with lower prices, hotels take a kindly attitude to traveling families and Oslo even has two museums dedicated to children.

- **Constitution Day** It's not exactly a holiday specifically for children, but it comes close, Norway's national day, 17 May, is dedicated to families and children and Oslo celebrates this event with a Children's Parade and light-hearted, family-oriented activities such as games and face painting.

- **The Children's Art Museum (Internasjonale Barnekunsmuseet)** Children's art from 180 countries. See page 102.

- **TusnFryd** is an amusement park about 10 km (6 miles) south of Oslo on Highway E6. It has rides, including carousels and a roller coaster, as well as swimming, and a fantasy farm.  The

TusenFrryd bus departs from the Galleri Oslo bus terminal nine times daily from 10.00 to 16.00.

- **Holmenkollen**, the most visited tourist attraction in Norway, is a favourite with young visitors. Climb to the top of the ski jump tower, tour the ski museum, have lunch in the cafeteria and visit the souvenir shop. See page 100.

- **Norwegian Folk Museum** Norway's largest open-air museum, with more than 140 buildings from all around the country. You can stroll the streets of 17th century village, peek inside a 12th century church or roam the grounds of a 19th century farm. From July to mid-August there are the Norwegian evenings of folk tales and folk dancing. See page 92.

- **Akershus Castle** For your future knight or damsel-in-distress in training, a few hours spent in the castle, with its dungeons and banquet rooms, will have them dreaming of days of old. There's even a drawbridge at the entrance. See page 69.

- **Beaches** Another good summertime treat is to head for the beach. All of us enjoy a few hours with a bucket and spade at the water's edge. The Bygdøy Peninsula has two popular beaches, Huk and Paradisbukta, that can be easily reached by bus. See page 97.

COMMUNICATIONS
Phones
The telephone system in Norway is very good, and quite extensive. Norway uses eight digit numbers with no area codes. Long-distance rates in Norway are among the lowest in the world. Local calls from

hotel rooms and pay phones cost 5Kr. Newsstands, post offices and railway stations sell telephone cards (TeleKort). Some pay phones accept credit cards. Faxes can be received or sent from most major hotels, although it is much cheaper to send them from a post office.

European and others with GSM mobile telephones should find that they work in Norway (North American cell phones will not). Norwegian SIM cards are available, but the instructions are in Norwegian, so you might want to purchase the card directly from Telehuset, who will connect you when you buy the card: Cards are also available at 7-Eleven stores, and at some Narvesen kiosks. Cards start at 200Kr, with 100Kr. worth of calls.

To call to Norway, dial your home country's international access code (usually 00), then Norway's country code, 47, plus the eight digit number. To call internationally from Norway, dial 00 plus your own country's code and then the area code and number (in UK area codes, omit the initial 0). Country codes include: UK 44, Republic of Ireland 353, USA and Canada 1, Australia 61, New Zealand 64 and South Africa 27.

Telehuset Ⓦ www.telehuset.no

Post

The postal service in Norway is very good. Mail going to other parts of Europe takes 2–3 days, to North America about a week. Postage for letters and postcards to other parts of Europe costs about 10Kr, and to the rest of the world about 12Kr. Post offices normally open 09.00–17.00 weekdays, 09.00–13.00 Saturdays; some offices in Oslo stay open longer.

Internet

There are many internet cafés in Oslo. Deichmanske Bibliotek

(Municipal Library) (✉ Henrik Ibsens Gate 1), offers 30 minutes of free internet access; however, you will need to call ahead to reserve a time (☎ 23 43 29 00). There are other public libraries in the city that also offer internet access. Networld Internet Café has two locations, one at the bus terminal at the Central Railway Station, and another at the Grønland T-bane Station. Both have many terminals, as well as scanning, printing and copying.

ELECTRICITY

Norway uses 220 V, 50 Hz alternating current. Sockets take the standard Continental plug with two round prongs. British visitors will need a plug adaptor for appliances; other visitors, including from North America, will also need a transformer for the different voltage. Both aids are best purchased at home before travelling.

SMOKING REGULATIONS

Since June 2004, anti-smoking regulations have become quite restrictive in Norway. In general, smoking is not allowed in any public place or on any public transportation. Smoking is not allowed in restaurants, bars and pubs, even in outdoor areas if they face other public places. Many hotel rooms are now designated as non-smoking.

TRAVELLERS WITH DISABILITIES

Norway caters for travellers with disabilities better than most countries, and all new buildings are required to have wheelchair access. Most street crossings have ramps or low curbs, and crossing signals also produce audible sounds (long beeps for safe to cross, and short beeps when the signal is about to change). Many trains have spaces for wheelchairs. If you travel with a wheelchair have it

serviced before your departure and carry any essentials you may need to affect repairs. It is also a good idea to travel with any spares of special clothing or equipment that might be difficult to replace.

However, Oslo can still be a challenge for travellers with disabilities. The Norwegian Association for the Disabled is a good source of information on hotels, restaurants and tourist attractions that are equipped to receive disabled visitors. Tourist offices also can be especially helpful in determining if there is suitable accommodation in the area you wish to visit if you make your request in advance.

It's a good idea to double-check any information you receive, as some establishments will advertise services that are still to be implemented. Associations dealing with your particular disability can be excellent sources of information on conditions and circumstances in other countries. The following contacts may be helpful:

Norwegian Association for the Disabled Schweigaards Gate 12, Oslo. 22 17 02 55, www.nhf.no

Tripscope UK-based travellers. Alexandra House, Albany Road, Brentford, Middlesex TW8 0NE. 0845 758 5641. www.tripscope.org.uk

Irish Wheelchair Association Blackheath Drive, Clontarf, Dublin 3. 01 818 6400. www.iwa.ie

Society for the Advancement of Travelers with Handicaps (SATH) North American-based travellers. 347 5th Avenue, New York, NY 10016, USA. 212 447 7284. www.sath.org

Access-able www.access-able.com

Australian Council for Rehabilitation of the Disabled (ACROD) PO Box 60, Curtin, ACT 2605; Suite 103, 1st Floor, 1–5 Commercial Road, Kings Grove, 2208. 02 6282 4333. www.acrod.org.au

Disabled Persons Assembly New Zealand-based travellers. 4/173–175 Victoria Street, Wellington. 04 801 9100. www.dpa.org.nz

FURTHER INFORMATION
Tourist information
Oslo Tourist Office has branches conveniently located at Oslo S, the main railway station and by the Rådhus (city hall). It deals only with Oslo, and can sell you an Oslo Pass and arrange accommodation. 81 53 05 55 (call centre, 09.00–16.00). www.visitoslo.com

Oslo S Trafikanten Service Centre, Oslo-S, Jernbanetorget 1. Mon–Fri 07.00–20.00, Sat & Sun 08.00–20.00 in the summer; closes 18.00 on Sat & Sun in the winter.

Rådhus Fridtjof Nansens Plass 5. Entrance from Roald Amundsens Gate. Daily 09.00–19.00 Jun–Aug. Closes 17.00 in spring & autumn, 16.00 in winter.

Oslo Promotion Tourist Office is located near the Rådhus (Town Hall). The office publishes a guide to Oslo, and a monthly paper on 'What's On in Oslo'. It has good maps of the city and the transit system. The website is quite extensive. Fridtjof Nansens 5. 24 14 77 00. www.visitoslo.com 09.00–16.00 in winter, longer in summer.

Norwegian Tourist Board Their website is very comprehensive, with much practical information. www.visitnorway.com

Norway Post This paper's website gives up-to-the-minute Norwegian news in English. It emphasises culture and travel. www.norwaypost.no

Useful phrases

Although English is widely spoken in Norway, these words and phrases may come in handy. See also the phrases for specific situations in other parts of the book.

English	Norwegian	Approx. pronunciation
BASICS		
Yes	Ja	Yah
No	Nei	Nay
Please	Vær så snill	Va sho snil
Thank you	Takk	Terk
Hello	Goddag	Gerdahg
Goodbye	Ha det	Hah deh
Excuse me	Unnskyld meg	Unshewl mey
Sorry	Beklager	Beh-klah-gehr
That's okay	Ingen årsak	Ing-en or-shahk
To	Til	Til
From	Fra	Fra
Do you speak English	Snakker du engelsk?	Snerkur doo ehng-erlsk?
Good morning	God morgen	Goo morrgon
Good afternoon	Goddag	Good-dahg
Good evening	God kveld	Goo kvehl
Goodnight	God natt	Goo nert
My name is ...	Jeg heter	Yeh hehterr

English	Norwegian	Approx. pronunciation
DAYS & TIMES		
Monday	mandag	merndahg
Tuesday	tirsdag	teeshdahg
Wednesday	onsdag	unsdahg
Thursday	torsdag	tooshdahg
Friday	fredag	frehdahg
Saturday	lørdag	lerdahg
Sunday	søndag	serndahg
Morning	Formiddag	Formiddahg
Afternoon	Ettermiddag	Ehtermiddahg
Night	Natt	Nert
Yesterday	Igår	Iggorr
Today	I dag	Iddahg

USEFUL PHRASES

English	Norwegian	Approx. pronunciation
Tomorrow	I morgen	Immorn
What time is it?	Hva er klokka?	Vah arr klokker?
It is ...	Klokka er ...	Klokker arr ...
09.00	Klokka er ni om formiddagen	Klokker nee um formiddahgen
Midday	Klokka tolv	Kloker tol
Midnight	Midtnatt	Mit-nert

NUMBERS

One	En	Ehn
Two	To	Too
Three	Tre	Treh
Four	Fire	Feerer
Five	Fem	Fehm
Six	Seks	Sehks
Seven	Sju	Shoo
Eight	Åtte	Otter
Nine	Ni	Nee
Ten	Ti	Tee
Twenty	Tjue	Chewer
Fifty	Femti	Fehmti
One hundred	Hundre	Hundrer
One thousand	Tusen	Tusern

MONEY

I would like to change these traveller's cheques/this currency	Jeg vil gjerne veksle reisesjekker/penger	Yeh vil yehrner vehksler rehser-shehker/pehng-er
What's the exchange rate?	Hva er valutakursen?	ah ar verlooter-kooshen?
Credit Cards	Kredittkort	Krehditkort

SIGNS & NOTICES

Airport	Lufthavn
Smoking/non-smoking	Røykning/Røykning forbudt
Toilets	Toaletter
Ladies/Gentlemen	Damer/Herrer
Open/Closed	Åpen/Stengt

8153

Emergencies

EMERGENCY TELEPHONE NUMBERS
Ambulance and other medical emergencies 113
Police 112
Fire 110
City Police 02800 or 22 66 90 50

MEDICAL EMERGENCIES
Doctors
If you become ill or injured while in Norway, your hotel can refer you to a local doctor, nearly all of whom speak English. If you are not staying at a hotel, call the national 24-hour emergency medical number, 113.

Accidents
Oslo kommunale legevakt (Public emergency ward) ⓐ Storgata 40. ⓘ 23 48 70 00. ⓦ www.oslolegevakt.no ⓛ Daily 24 hours, including public holidays. ⓣ Tram or bus: Hausmanns gate.

Pharmacies
Pharmacies are open during normal shopping hours, and some are also open weekends and evenings for emergencies. If you should become ill during a trip to Norway, the staff at your hotel will normally be able to put you in touch with a local doctor or the emergency medical service. If you use any prescription drugs, be sure to bring enough to last for your entire stay in Norway. Norwegian pharmacies are not permitted to give out medicine on prescriptions from outside of the country, and if you do run short, you will need to contact a Norwegian doctor in order to get a

prescription for a new supply. There is a 24-hour pharmacy near the central station:

Jernbanetorvet Pharmacy ⓐ Jernbanetorget 4B ⓣ 23 35 81 00 ⓦ www.vitus.no ⓛ Daily 24 hours, including public holidays. ⓝ Tram: Jernbanetorget/Oslo S.

Dental emergencies

Tannlegevakten Oslo public emergency dental clinic at Tøyen. Not possible to make appointments – show up in person. For children and adults. Minimum fee: 399Kr. (cash only) for a 10-minute consultancy, ⓐ Kolstadgata 18. ⓣ 22 67 30 00 ⓛ Mon–Fri 19.00–22.00, Sat–Sun 11.00–14.00. ⓝ T-bane: Tøyen .

POLICE STATION

Oslo Police District ⓐ Politihuset, Grønlandsleiret 44. ⓣ 02800 or 22 66 90 50.

EMERGENCY PHRASES

Help! Hjelp! *Yehlp!*

Call an ambulance/Call a doctor/Call the police!
Ring etter en sykebil/Ring en lege/Ring politiet!
Ring ehtterehn sewkerbeel/Ring ehn lehger/Ring pulitee-er!

Can you help me please?
Kan du hjelpe meg, kanskje?
Kern doo yehlper meh, koonsher?

LOST PROPERTY
Police ☎ 22 66 98 65.
Trams, buses, T-bane (Oslo Sporveier) ☎ 22 08 53 61.
Railway (NSB - Oslo Central Station) ☎ 23 15 00 00.

Reporting lost or stolen credit cards:
American Express ☎ 80 06 81 00.
Diners Club ☎ 23 00 10 00.
Eurocard ☎ 22 98 12 50.
Mastercard ☎ 80 03 02 50.
Visa ☎ 81 50 05 00.

EMBASSIES & CONSULATES
Australia Embassy is closed in Oslo; contact the embassy in
Denmark ◉ Dampfaergevej 26, Second Floor, Copenhagen DK-2100.
☎ +45 7026 3686.
Canada ◉ Wergelandsveien 7, Oslo. ☎ 22 99 53 00.
New Zealand Consulate, ◉ Billingstadsletta 19B, P.O. Box 113,
Billingstad N-1376. ☎ 66 77 53 30.
South Africa Embassy ◉ Drammensveien 88 c, Oslo.
☎ 09 47 2327 3220.
United Kingdom Embassy. ◉ Thomas Heftyes Gate 8, Oslo.
☎ 23 13 27 00.
United States Embassy. ◉ Drammensveien 18, Oslo. ☎ 22 44 85 50.

◗ *Oslo is one of the world's safest and most relaxed destinations*

INDEX

The publishers would like to thank the following individuals and organisations for supplying their copyright photographs for this book.
A1 Pix: pages 1 and 68.
Nancy Bundt: pages 5, 9, 13, 17, 21, 29, 32, 39, 40, 42, 61, 63, 75, 81, 113, and 133. Nancy Bundt/Innovation Norway: pages 31, 85, 89, 107, 111, 129 and 157.
Stillman Rogers Photography: pages 7, 18, 25, 45, 47, 93, 95, 96, 98, 101, 103, 117, 121, 124 and 141.

Proofreader: Angela Chevalier-Watts
Copy-editor: Stephen York

Send your thoughts to
books@thomascook.com

- Found a great bar, club, shop or must-see sight that we don't feature?

- Like to tip us off about any information that needs a little updating?

- Want to tell us what you love about this handy little guidebook and more importantly how we can make it even handier?

Then here's your chance to tell all! Send us ideas, discoveries and recommendations today and then look out for your valuable input in the next edition of this title. As an extra 'thank you' from Thomas Cook Publishing, you'll be automatically entered into our exciting monthly prize draw.

Email the above address (stating the book's title) or write to: CitySpots Project Editor, Thomas Cook Publishing, PO Box 227, Unit 15/16, Coningsby Road, Peterborough PE3 8SB, UK.

SPOT THE DIFFERENCE

SKI SPOTS
ANDORRA

including
Pal–Arinsal, Ordino–Arcalís,
Soldeu–El Tarter, Pas de la Casa–Grau Roig

HOT SPOTS
EGYPT
RED SEA RESORTS

Soma Bay, Makadi Bay, Hurghada, El Gouna,
Marsa Alam, Sharm el Sheikh

With these brand new guides from Thomas
Cook Publishing you'll pocket all the
information you need for a relaxing beach break
in some of the world's best known resorts or an
exhilarating snowsports holiday at some of the
most popular ski areas in Europe. Maps,
restaurants, attractions, transport, nightlife and
much, much more to make your stay spot on!
With over thirty HotSpots and SkiSpots in the
series, we'll guide you to a better holiday
around the world.

CITY**SPOTS**
OSLO

Perfect for pleasure-seeking city breakers this pocket guide quickly pinpoints Oslo's most entertaining highlights and helps you decide what to see and do in a limited time. Capturing the spirit of the Norwegian capital, our writer introduces must-see sights such as Vigeland Sculpture Park as well as offering the lowdown on the city's fifty-plus museums, its fantastic scenery, non-stop nightlife and much more.

Including:
- Central Oslo, Grunerlokka, Gronland & Bygdøy Peninsula
- Out-of-town trips to Bergen & the fjords

ISBN 978-1-84157-585-8
ISBN 1-84157-585-2

9 781841 575858

UK £5.99
US $10.95

Thomas Cook
Publishing
www.thomascookpublishing.com